How To Books on Successful Writing

Copyright & Law for Writers
Creating a Twist in the Tale
How to Be a Freelance Journalist
How to Publish a Book
How to Publish a Newsletter
How to Start Word Processing
How to Write a Press Release
How to Write a Report
How to Write an Assignment
How to Write & Sell Computer
  Software
How to Write for Publication
How to Write for Television
How to Write Your Dissertation
Mastering Business English
Starting to Write
Writing a Nonfiction Book
Writing an Essay
Writing & Selling a Novel
Writing & Selling Short Stories
Writing Business Letters
Writing Reviews

Other titles in preparation

The How To Series now contains more than 200 titles in the following categories:

Business Basics
Family Reference
Jobs & Careers
Living & Working Abroad
Student Handbooks
Successful Writing

Please send for a free copy of the latest catalogue for full details (see back cover for address).

SUCCESSFUL WRITING

WRITING A NONFICTION BOOK

How to prepare your work for publication

Norman Toulson

How To Books

Cartoons by Mike Flanagan

British Library Cataloguing in Publication Data
A catalogue record for this book is available from the British Library.

© Copyright 1997 by Norman Toulson.

First published in 1997 by How To Books Ltd, 3 Newtec Place,
Magdalen Road, Oxford OX4 1RE, United Kingdom.
Tel: (01865) 793806. Fax: (01865) 248780.

Note: The material contained in this book is set out in good faith for general
guidance and no liability can be accepted for loss or expense incurred as a
result of relying in particular circumstances on statements made in this book.
The laws and regulations may be complex and liable to change, and readers
should check the current position with the relevant authorities before making
personal arrangements.

Produced for How To Books by Deer Park Productions.
Typeset by Concept Communications (Design & Print) Ltd, Crayford, Kent.
Printed and bound by Cromwell Press, Broughton Gifford, Melksham, Wiltshire.

Contents

List of Illustrations

Preface

'You will have written exceptionally well if, by skilful
arrangement of your words, you have made an ordinary
one seem original.'

Those words were written by the Roman poet, Horace, more than
2,000 years ago. Nobody will be reading this book in 2,000 years'
time. But it may help *you* to see a book *you* have written, in print and
on a shelf in a bookshop, this year or next year.

You would not be reading this preface unless you wanted to see
something you had written published. You may not be sure whether
you want to write stories, articles, novels or non-fiction books.
Although the purpose of the book is to help you with the last of these
four groups, some of the advice can help you with any of them.

It is common practice for legal documents to include some such
statement as 'In the interpretation of this document, the masculine
shall be deemed to include the feminine, and the singular to include
the plural, and vice versa'. This is not a legal document. It occasionally
uses the expression 'he or she' and 'him and her'. Any omission to
do so, where appropriate, is accidental. Members of both sexes make
valuable contributions to our literature, both fiction and non-fiction.

References to 'the publisher', in this book, usually refer to the
individual, partnership or limited company that owns the publishing
business with which the reader is negotiating or has a contract.
Occasionally it refers to the individual who is dealing with the reader,
on behalf of the publisher.

Whether you have been head-hunted to write your book or have an
urge to try your hand on a broader canvas than you have ever used
before, the author and the publisher hope they will help you to
succeed.

Norman Toulson

1
Looking at the Market

You want to write a book. You want to see it in print. You want people to buy it.

Unless you have several other skills, in addition to the ability to write well, you will need to persuade a publisher to put your manuscript into book form and to sell the book to the reading public. He or she will want to check not only that the book is well written but also that there is a market for it. And the market must not already be overloaded with competing books on the subject.

Do yourself a favour. Study the market for yourself before you go any further. What books can people already buy or borrow about your subject? Find out before you spend time planning to write something for a non-existent market. When you go looking for books about your subject, take a notebook with you.

LOCATING EXISTING BOOKS

Where do people get the books they read? They buy or borrow them.

Looking in bookshops

Which shops will give you the best view of what people are buying? For non-fiction you usually need to visit the shops with the largest stocks. In a village or small town the accent is likely to be on paperback fiction unless there is a non-fiction topic of special local interest. For example, the stock of any bookshop in Stratford-upon-Avon is likely to have a strongly Shakespearean flavour. The shop is unlikely to have anything about whale hunting in the southern hemisphere.

A university town usually has at least one bookshop that students patronise. That is where you will find the town's largest range of non-fiction books on sale.

The centre of a large city may have a professional enclave where lawyers, accountants and financial advisers have their offices. If so, a bookshop stocking textbooks about legal and financial matters is likely to be nearby. And selling medical textbooks may provide a healthy income for a shop near a large teaching hospital.

Before leaving a shop, spare a few moments for the bargain offers tables. If you do see the kind of book you are looking for there, try to find out why the shop has slashed the price. Was there no demand for the subject or has a new book superseded this one? The publication date may give you a clue.

Looking in public libraries

These are the most important other places for you to visit in your research of the market. Public libraries may become your best customers. Nationwide, they buy millions of books each year.

Even if the local branch of your county library is a small one, it can help you as much as any part of the county network, if it has a copy of the **county catalogue**. This lists all the books held by all the branches in the county and consists of three elements:

- an index to the numerical classifications of subjects
- a file of microfiches
- a viewer.

The index is alphabetical and is usually divided into several volumes, such as A-D, E-K, L-R and S-Z. A typical entry is shown in Figure 1.

Pensions – Civil Service

– central governments		351.5
– employment law		344.01252
"	***	344.012
– executive management		658.407253
"	***	658.407
– labour economics		331.252
– social security		368.43

*** old numbers – no longer used

Fig. 1. Specimen entry in index of numerical classifications of subjects.

If you wanted to discover what books about pension schemes were held in your county's libraries, you would need to remove the **microfiche** that included classification 331.252 from the file and insert it in the viewer. Each microfiche contains details in minute letters and numerals of a large number of books.

Figure 2 shows an example of the information recorded about one title under subject 331.252 on a microfiche in the catalogue for Kent County Library.

Toulson Norman		331.252
The Pensions Revolution: An Employer's Guide		PBK
Kogan Page	1988	88/32
1850917647		
Dover A	Maidstone A	T Wells A
Tonbridge R		

The ten digit number is the International Standard Book Number. The information in the subsequent lines indicates the branch libraries that hold copies of the book. The letter 'R' indicates that the copy at Tonbridge library is in the reference section and not available for borrowing. It can be referred to only in the reading room.

Fig. 2. Specimen microfiche information in Kent County Library catalogue.

As you look at the entries relating to your subject on a microfiche, note the details of any book you would like to examine. If neither your local library nor any other easily accessible branch has a copy, you can arrange for your local library to borrow a copy from another branch. A small fee will be charged.

Borrowing a book may help you more than thumbing through a copy in the library. Examining it at leisure, at home, enables you to make notes of various items that may prove useful as you proceed with your research.

Finding other libraries
If your searches in bookshops and public libraries unearth less information than you hoped for, you might find books about your subject

in a privately owned library. A phone call to the librarian may tell you whether:

- the library has relevant books
- you could have access to them.

Examples of such libraries are those of:

- universities
- schools
- learned societies
- professional associations
- trade associations.

The existence of a book in a private library, but not in public libraries, is unlikely to constitute competition for anything you may write. It may give a clue to how long has elapsed since a book on the subject was published.

SEEING WHAT THE BOOKS COVER

At which kinds of reader did the authors of the books you have seen aim their work? Some readers are happy to glean a few facts; others want to know the whys and wherefores. Neither group would be happy with a book designed to attract the other. So each group is a different market.

The length of a book is not, by itself, a reliable criterion by which to assess its readership. Two books of the same length on the same subject may differ greatly in style. An author who uses simple terms to explain a simple process to a novice reader usually uses many short sentences and paragraphs. But he or she covers far less ground in 100 pages than somebody who aims to meet the needs of advanced students.

Noting how authors handle their material can help you when you come to plan your own work. Their division of the subject into chapters and sections, and the sequence in which they deal with its various aspects, may differ greatly. Comparing the differences in their approaches could help you to adopt a better layout than you had in mind.

To the extent to which you will be competing with other authors, you need to deal with the subject better than they do. Let their excellence spur you to achieve perfection.

FINDING OTHER VALUABLE CLUES

Microfiches and the publisher's notes at the beginning of a book may contain useful information you could easily overlook. They may tell you about the author's other books. Does this lady also write about other subjects? Does she write about this subject every three years? If so, is her next book due in the next six months? If it is, the prospects for a book by you might be far from bright.

And take a look at the gummed slip immediately inside each library book – the one that lists the dates on which successive borrowers were due to return the book. The frequency of the dates gives a clue to the popularity of the book. But if the sequence ended a couple of years ago, another book has probably taken this one's place.

Alternatively, interest in the subject may have waned. Try to compare the dates in another book on the subject. Be alert to put two and two together to make four.

NOTING TARGET MARKETS

Collating all the facts your research has found should give you a valuable pointer to the degree of interest people show in your subject and whether the time is ripe for you to write another book about it. You have learned when the existing books were written. Your knowledge of the subject will tell you whether a change in legislation, methods of production, people's habits or any other factor has made those books obsolete. If it has, the sooner you draft an up-to-date book the better.

On the other hand, even if nothing significant has happened to make the books out-of-date, you may believe that a book written with a lighter touch or in contemporary language would appeal more to the public. You may be right.

Or something in the news may have reawakened public interest in a subject that had attracted little attention in recent years. A new book about it might find a ready market. If you wrote it, you could be backing a winner.

FINDING A NICHE

Seeing and seizing an opportunity is a recipe for success for an author as well as for a burglar – and far more laudable.

But where in the market for a book about your chosen subject should you aim to find your readers? Will they be in schools or universities? Will they be working at lathes or pushing pens? Will they be in their 20s or their 70s?

Define the reader you want to attract as clearly as you can. Otherwise you may begin to feel like the anti-aircraft gunner who, after an air raid on London in World War 2, said he had been firing at nothing all night, and hitting it every time.

While you were studying the demand and the books already on offer, did you notice any part of the potential readership for whom nobody had written about the subject? For example, you may have been looking at books for people who are leaving full-time education and want to enter a particular career. Would those books help someone who had been forced to leave that career for family reasons, several years ago, but wanted to take it up again? And would the books help a redundant older person who would like to adopt this as a new career? If not, would there be a demand for a book designed to deal with either or both of those situations? It might be more rewarding in every way for you to write such a book than to compete with the books already written for people who are leaving school or higher education.

Your eventual choice of niche may differ greatly from your original concept. It may also contain few of the other ideas that have jockeyed with each other in your mind while you were researching the market. That is fine. It is better to have second and third thoughts at this stage than when you are halfway through drafting the book.

CHECKLIST

● How many relevant books did you find in shops and libraries?

● How many were up-to-date?

● Who were they aimed at?

● Who else needs them?

● Which gap should you aim to fill?

CASE STUDIES

To help you to apply what you have been reading, here are brief details of four people who want to write non-fiction books, and their progress so far. At the end of each subsequent chapter you will see what further progress they are making.

Betty manages a photographic shop

Betty is a 27-year-old divorcee with a six-year-old daughter and a lively sense of the ridiculous. She manages a photographic equipment shop. She entered the business in her teens and quickly developed a flair for cameracraft. She learned not only from her colleagues but also from those customers who were winning prizes with their hobby.

She has amassed a collection of her own pictures that tickle people's chuckle muscles. She would like to use many of them to illustrate a book with some such title as *Hilarious Holidays with a Camera*. She believes that it could appeal to casual snappers as well as people who study books about camera techniques. She would also like to write the text of the book.

She explores the shelves of her nearest branches of W H Smith and Waterstones and visits a shop that specialises in books for students of visual art. She finds nothing on the lines she has been planning. Similarly she draws a blank when she visits public libraries. The nearest she finds is books showing cats in odd situations and other droll animal pictures. While hesitating to think her idea is unique, she believes she faces no direct competition. She accepts that this does not guarantee that she will find a ready market for her work.

Charles is taking a gap year

Charles is taking a year off from studying, before going to university. He would like to devote part of it to walking round England – preferably with a companion. His objectives are to discipline himself to carrying out the self-imposed task, and to raise sponsorship money for a charity. He would also like to write a book about the journey, both as a second challenge and as a second source of money for the charity.

He finds, in both bookshops and libraries, that several people have written about treks on foot or on wheeled vehicles, on boats or on sledges. From what he has seen on the date stamps in library books, he has guessed that the author's ability to excite the reader's imagination matters more than choosing a way-out itinerary for the journey. He suspects that a humorous description of a stroll round Kensington Gardens would attract more readers than a statistical analysis of an expedition across the Sahara Desert on a camel.

Margaret plans to write geography books

Margaret is 30 years old and teaches geography to teenagers. During her holidays she has visited countries in all the non-polar continents. She would like to use the experience she has gained to write one or more books that would help to bring her subject to life for children in other schools as well as the one in which she teaches.

She has looked at several geography textbooks, searching for the kind of presentation she has in mind. She feels that their authors often fail to link the facts they quote about other countries with what students see of them in news and travel programmes on TV. On her trips abroad, she has been more concerned with seeing the everyday lives of the local people than with visiting bathing beaches. She is sure that her holiday experiences enable her to inject life into the syllabus and to act as a catalyst between her pupils' schoolroom studies and their TV viewing.

Tony volunteers to write a history of his company

Tony is manager of the publicity department of a life assurance company. He was head-hunted for the job from a firm of publicity consultants. The company is nearing the 150th anniversary of the day when it was founded. The board of directors wants to publish a history of the company, as part of the celebrations, and has asked Tony to arrange for somebody to write it. The titbits he has heard and read about the company's early days have fascinated him. He volunteers to write the book himself, and the board approves.

He looks at similar ventures by other companies. He thinks that most of them lack sparkle. He wants to write a book that people will enjoy reading.

Putting it on a shelf as a status symbol will achieve little for the company. People who receive copies should find them compelling reading. They should want to quote bits to other people and talk about them to their friends. That would be good publicity for the company. That is what a publicity manager should be looking for.

DISCUSSION POINTS

1.   Have you looked critically at all the competing books you have seen and noted their good and bad points?

2.   Which author threatens the strongest competition? Could you slant your ideas to avoid competing head-on?

3.   Can you find two niches, so that you could write a second book to establish yourself in the market?

2
Planning the Scope of the Book

In *Alice in Wonderland*, the King said, 'Begin at the beginning and go on till you come to the end: then stop'. That may be how some people write short stories successfully. It would not be good advice to the authors of many non-fiction books. Before putting pen to paper or disk into personal computer, they need to decide where their books should begin and end, and what they should include in between.

PICTURING THE READER

People who are learning to speak in public are sometimes advised to pick one member of the audience and address what they have to say to that person. It may help you to plan and write your book if you picture one person whom you expect to read your book, and have an image of that person in your mind. The following subsection suggests how you might do this. Skip it if you do not need it.

Creating an image

Choose somebody who you know is interested in your subject, or is learning about it, if you can. If no real person springs to mind, you can invent one, but be sure that you believe in the fictitious guinea pig you choose. He or she will have no value otherwise. Build up a **personality**. The draft form in Figure 3 shows you how you might do this.

Do all the details you have entered in the form fit in with somebody with an interest in the subject? If not, alter them. Create a credible image of somebody you are going to sell your book to. You might find a picture in a newspaper or magazine that resembles your image. Cut it out and pin it to the form. It will help to bring your image to life.

Another possibility would be to go to a bookshop or library and watch somebody picking up a book on your subject and glancing through the pages. There, surely, you would have a real potential reader to capture on your form.

19

Name		Age	Sex
Married/single/widow/divorced/separated			
Number of children			
Types of school reader attended			
Full-time further education			
Evening classes *etc.*			
Academic degrees, diplomas *etc*			
Occupation			
Employee/self-employed			
Previous occupations			
Ambitions			
Recreations			
Hobbies			
Political persuasion			
Religious persuasion			
Other information			

Fig. 3. Data relating to a target reader – real or imaginary.

CONSIDERING WHAT TO COVER

● Where would you draw your boundaries?

● Where should you begin and end?

● What should you include in between?

● What would your target reader expect you to cover?

● Would he or she be satisfied with what you have in mind?

Try to picture yourself in the days before you first read a book about the subject. Would what you propose to do have satisfied your demand for knowledge?

If you want your book to serve as a textbook for students who will be sitting an exam, you must be sure you know the current syllabus. Study it in detail. It should tell you, in outline, what you need to include.

Usually you will have no such blueprint. Whether you have

chosen the subject yourself or have been asked to write about it, you need to decide or agree its length, breadth and depth.

How much should you expect readers to know before they open the book? Newcomers to the subject may drown in a flood of unfamiliar language if you throw them in at the deep end. On the other hand, people who are eager to increase their grasp of the subject may resent finding themselves taken back to first principles.

It would be a pity to exclude either group from the potential market for your book. It would be worse to try to satisfy both and fail to attract either, as a result. If you knew which would be likely to be the more profitable group, prudence might suggest you should jettison the other.

Adopting a flexible approach

There is another possibility. Editors of magazines that use serial stories put a 'New readers start here' panel at the beginning of each instalment. If you devoted your first chapter to a recap of what many possible readers already knew, you could enable comparative novices to understand the book. A note at the beginning of the chapter could state that it was an introduction to the subject, for the benefit of readers who were new to it, and that some readers might prefer to go straight to Chapter 2.

Knowing where to finish

Having chosen your starting line, you need to decide where to draw your finishing line. If your subject is in any sense a history, either of a group of people or of an activity or process of some kind, your arrival at the present day will dictate the end of the story. (A look at the future may be in order, but it may be a relatively brief coda or epilogue.)

Other kinds of subject can be more realistic. Theoretically a cookery book might go on and on for ever. Before the author has exhausted the recipes of cooks from all over the world, another generation would have replaced them in their kitchens.

In practice, if your subject has no historical limit, the length of your book will depend on how deeply you delve and how concisely you write. So how deeply do you expect your readers to want to go?

As long as you are making the book more valuable to some of them, you may be increasing the scope for selling it. But if your deeper coverage of the subject makes the book less attractive to the average reader, you do yourself a disservice by going on.

Answer each question fully before passing to the next.
Amend a question to fit your subject, rather than skip it.
Refrain from putting N/A (not applicable) without due thought.

What changes have there been since you learned your job or
passed your final exam? _____
_____
_____

How has the law changed in relation to your occupation? ____
_____
_____

How have ways of doing things changed? _____
_____
_____

How have customers' preferences changed? _____
_____
_____

Which manufacturing processes have become obsolete? ____
_____
_____

What new processes have been introduced? _____
_____
_____

How are the systems you use in your business out of line with
the rest of the industry? _____
_____
_____

What was that discovery somebody made, last month, that
you meant to make a note of? _____
_____
_____

Today's date _____

Fig. 4. Analysis of matters on which you need to update your knowledge.

Benefiting from rivals' experience

Before making a decision about the scope of the book, spend a little time in examining competing books on your subject. You have no wish to copy them, of course. (You will never be a leader, as long as you follow other people.) But you may spot something valuable that you had left out of account in your planning. Be glad you have found it before you would need to make a major change in the text to include it.

REVIEWING YOUR OWN KNOWLEDGE

How much do you know about all that you have decided your book ought to cover? Could you give a series of talks about it, confident that you could answer every serious question the audience might ask you?

Think about each of these questions in detail. Apply them to every aspect of the subject. Put the brakes on if you find yourself dismissing any item without due thought.

Do you fully understand it or is it one of the parts about which you hoped there would be no question in your exam, when you were studying the subject? Be honest with yourself. Perhaps you were able to skip it, because the examiners required you to answer only six questions out of eight. If it has cropped up since then, you may have dealt with it by quoting parrot-fashion something you had read.

The time has come for you to come clean with yourself. You need to master that grey area, so that you can talk and write about it in simple language. Encourage yourself by assuming that your readers will find it difficult, too. Make up your mind to find a way to deal with it. You will make it so simple that all of your readers will grasp it. When you achieve that, you will take a large stride forward in your progress as an author.

Updating yourself

Your knowledge needs to be up-to-date. Make a large copy of the questionnaire in Figure 4 and answer it before going any further with the planning of your book. It will give you an idea of where you need to update yourself.

The kinds of changes you need to look for will vary from one subject to another. A book about shoeing horses dates far less quickly than one about taxation.

Make careful notes of all the areas where you ought to check, update or extend your knowledge. Keep the notes handy and add to them whenever you call another point to mind.

Keep a **jotter** and a **pencil** in your pocket. The moment you think of another item, write it down. That phone call will have to wait for a moment or two. You may have forgotten the item by the time the call ends. You want the list to be complete. Any attempt to compile it at one fell swoop is bound to fail.

And remember to make a note of any projected change of law or practice that will take effect by the time your book is published.

PLANNING FURTHER RESEARCH

After allowing a reasonable time for the completion of your notes, sift through them. Eliminate any duplicates, and merge details that overlap. List the items that remain on a chart such as that in Figure 5.

Knowledge needing update	Official handouts *etc*	Trade/professional Journals *etc*	Seminars conferences *etc*	Other sources

Fig. 5. Possible sources for updating knowledge.

Add to the items in the first column any other matters that need to be explained because of a recent or impending change. For example, if a process related to the subject is being automated, you may need to learn the background to the particular method of automation.

Filling the gaps

How are you going to fill the gaps in your knowledge of the subject? There is no standard answer. The resources that are available differ greatly between one subject and another.

It might seem that a book with which yours will compete is the most obvious place to look. Its publication date will suggest how likely the information in it is to be up-to-date. If you know the author, either directly or by repute, you may have an indication of his or her reliability. But beware of being too trusting! Nobody is infallible. If you follow an inaccurate source, you carry the can.

Refer to original sources, wherever possible. It is not unknown for two or more authors to rely on the same faulty source for their information.

Finding original sources

What are original sources? As far as law is concerned, Acts of Parliament and Statutory Instruments are the main authorities. Wading through them is no picnic, but journals for members of various occupations contain articles that draw attention to relevant changes in the law and explain them. If they are written by lawyers who work closely with people in the occupations concerned, they should be as good as original sources.

Occupational journals also contain news of many other kinds of developments that interest readers. These can range from archaeological research that throws new light on how our ancestors lived (which interests historians) to new equipment for packaging perishable foods (which interests wholesale grocers).

If the journals contain articles written by people who designed or played an important part in the developments, these are effectively original sources.

But information is not all stored in books, journals, videotapes and other means of recording it. Much is locked away in the memories of people who have been concerned with creating or collecting it. Seize any opportunity you have of meeting them or hearing them talk about your subject. Word of mouth can be the best original source, if you know the reliability of the mind and memory behind the mouth.

FINDING ADDITIONAL RESEARCH FACILITIES

You may want to delve into the origins of long-established practices or restrictions that concern your subject in some way. For example, why is a standard component in a piece of equipment always X centimetres long? Where might you find out?

Are there any specialist journals that relate, in any way, to your subject? If there are, you might usefully spend a few hours searching through back numbers. A letter to the publishers of the journals, asking for permission to see their bound volumes, for research purposes, may bring a favourable reply.

To anybody who is concerned with writing books, the most obvious place in which to seek knowledge is a library. But which library should you consult?

Your local public library may be adequate, particularly if it contains a reference department as well as a lending department. The county library catalogue may list other books you could order through your local branch. If you suspect that even that resource falls short of what must be available somewhere, what do you do?

Chapter 1 mentions library facilities in connection with trying to find out what competition you would be up against if you wrote a book. Now you are interested in them as sources of information for you to include in your book. The Useful Addresses and Further Reading sections of this book contain details of *The Writer's Handbook*. Its contents include a section listing more than 100 libraries in the UK. You ought to find somewhere helpful among them.

CHECKLIST

● How do you picture your reader and his/her background?

● What length, breadth and depth does this suggest for your book?

● What gaps in your knowledge of the subject are there?

● How do you intend to fill those gaps?

● Where and how will you find the material recorded?

● What other locations do you intend to visit?

● What individuals, if any, do you intend to consult?

CASE STUDIES

Betty thinks about her writing style
Betty sees her target reader as someone in their 30s or 40s who chooses a newspaper more by reference to the subtlety of its cryptic cartoons than by its page three girls.

She has sorted her amusing pictures into groups and found that some groups are far larger than others. She has noted the smaller groups, and is giving some thought to possible ways of expanding them. Also she appreciates that the text of the chapters that will provide settings for the photographs needs to match them for humour. With this in mind, she plans to devote some of her leisure reading to humorous books of various styles. She believes that this will help her to write in lighter vein than she has been used to. She does not intend to try to copy anybody else's style. She hopes to pick up clues from what she reads, and to develop a style of her own. She also intends to add to her stock of pictures.

Charles aims at the nostalgia market

Charles sees his target reader as an armchair explorer who enjoys reading about other people's travels to places he is unlikely to ever visit himself. He is probably in his 70s or 80s and may have gone on walking holidays with one or more companions, in his teens and 20s, sleeping at youth hostels. He has heard more than enough about globe-trotters jetting to far countries. That is a world he does not know. He wants to revel in nostalgia as he reads about somebody half a century younger than him who is still happy to explore England by shanks's pony.

Charles accepts that he and his companion will need to plan the route of their trek in advance. They will want to study guide books to locate places of interest that lie near to the appropriate tracks and footpaths, so that they can visit them. They will also want to keep a record of their daily progress, in notebooks or on tapes. These will provide the raw material for the book. And before starting out they should find out how best to use photography to illustrate the book.

Should they take prints or transparencies? Do they need an SLR camera, or can they rely on a modest auto-focus, pocket size, no-nonsense job?

Margaret focuses on Australia

Margaret can easily picture her reader. She sees him/her every day in the classroom. She can visualise several readers, of various abilities. She can assess their likely interest in and grasp of what she might write.

She would like to start by writing about Australia. She has not only visited the country twice but also explored several parts of it during a long stay with a cousin who lives there. She brought back several guide books to keep her memory fresh. She corresponds regularly with the cousin, who would happily collect and send her publicity handouts on any subject about which she wanted to update herself.

Tony plans his research

Tony knows that copies of the book will be distributed to all the staff of the company and to independent financial advisers throughout the UK. He has met a sizeable sample of both these groups and knows what diverse interests they have. He wants to include material to capture the attention of all the prospective readers.

He knows that he must open with a sentence that will make everybody sit up and take notice before he begins to explain, in language that compels interest, how the company started. He will keep on the alert for that key item, as he searches for the material for the book.

He will also need to describe how the company developed, what important changes it has made and where it stands today. He has read the book the company published to mark its centenary and he has learned a great deal about recent developments from talking to members of the staff. He has been shown the archives, including board minute books dating back to the first meeting.

He intends to talk to pensioners and long-serving members of the staff, and probe their memories for quotable incidents. He also plans to visit libraries that have bound volumes of newspapers and magazines that contain references to the company – particularly its early days. To relate the company's progress to the economic climate in which it has operated, he plans to study a book about the social and economic history of the UK during the last 150 years.

DISCUSSION POINTS

1. Does the personality of the reader you are imagining cramp your coverage of the subject or give you too much scope?

2. Is your coverage inadequate for students sitting a relevant exam?

3. Have you clarified all the grey areas in your grasp of your subject?

4. Have you identified all the recent changes affecting your subject matter?

5. Have you noted any imminent changes relating to your subject?

3
Preparing a Synopsis

'If you haven't got a map, you might as well pack up before you start.' That is as true if you are embarking on writing a non-fiction book as it would be if you were setting out to walk across Dartmoor.

Having decided what your book is to contain and collected all the material you want to include in it, you need to prepare a map of your path from the beginning of Chapter 1 to the end of the book. It is called a **synopsis** and it will do more than help you to progress through your subject by a route a reader can follow. It will also help publishers to whom you submit your ideas for the book to assess whether it would suit their lists. Without a synopsis, they might well reject it out of hand. With a synopsis, they can see whether what you are offering may deserve encouraging.

The contents pages at the beginning of this book are an example of a synopsis.

STRUCTURING YOUR BOOK

Changing from a metaphor to a simile, one might say that preparing the map of your route is like solving a jigsaw puzzle. Whether you usually enjoy these puzzles or steer clear of them, you must have seen someone sorting the pieces before trying to fit them together in the right places.

Usually the first step is to pick out all the pieces for the framework and put it together. Then the remaining pieces are sorted by colour and other indications of the subject, and fitted into place.

You can use a similar system to sort all the material you have collected for your book. You group the items according to the section or aspect of your subject to which they relate. You may find it a good idea to write each item on a card, briefly, and sort the cards into heaps. The activity of allocating each card to one heap or another will help to clarify the subject in your mind.

If you prefer some other way of rough-sorting your data into handy groups, by all means use it.

USING A LOGICAL SEQUENCE

The next task is deciding which group of data should come first, which second and so on. Your book should lead a reader through the subject in a way that he or she will be able to follow easily. If readers find that a passage on page 12 baffles them until they are half-way through page 95, you have chosen the wrong sequence. You have failed to sort your material into a good order. Unfortunately this can happen. Be on your guard against it.

This does not mean that there is a unique right sequence for what you are going to tell your readers. You might be able to arrange your data in any of several ways with equal clarity. As long as your order suits your subject and your readers, you will be on safe ground.

LO I SEE ME AT A QUICK GLANCE

What on earth does that mean?
It's an anagram of

MAKE IT A LOGICAL SEQUENCE

Of course!

Fig. 6. Sorting it out.

Being better than merely safe

Your book may be competing with half a dozen others that are equally safely based. If you add something special that the others lack, you might earn a larger share of the market. That must be worth striving for. It would not only increase your immediate reward but also delight your publisher and encourage your readers to look out for other books written by you in the future.

How might you achieve this? If your book is in any sense describing an ongoing situation or process, you may be able to adopt a progressive set of semi-parallel chapters, like the 'meanwhile, back at the ranch' style used by some novelists. In such a book, the first chapter might describe Ian having a hectic day, trying to persuade a client to buy a £1M piece of plant; the domestic problems his wife is wrestling with, at the same time, occupy the second chapter.

You can fit the system to non-fiction. If you were writing about the history of a car manufacturer, you might devote one chapter to each new model the company offered to the market. That would be a traditional approach. Instead you could decide that successive chapters should detail chassis improvements from 1935 to 1948, engine developments from 1937 to 1949, and gearbox design achievements in the early 1950s. The repetitive theme would be, 'While that was going on at A, they were doing this that and the other at B'.

Suppose, instead, that you were planning to write *What You Should Know About The Law*. Traditionally you would probably have chapters on buying or renting a house, marriage and divorce, making and executing a will, and so on.

A different approach would be to start with 'rights and duties we all have'. From there you could look at the many incidents and accidents we all risk facing at some time in our lives. Explain in easy terms how the systems of the law operate. Take the reader into a court room, and take off the judge's wig and gown. Simplicity and humanity can carry you a long way.

Bear this in mind when you are looking at competing books. Make a note of the sequence of their chapters. Try to design something better than what you have seen. It may attract potential readers in your direction.

CHOOSING CHAPTER HEADINGS

Charles Dickens was a highly successful author but his chapter headings have little appeal to modern readers. He is said to have been paid by the yard for what he wrote. If so, his 40- or 50-word chapter headings must have boosted his pay cheque. They would put it in jeopardy today.

Being brief
Be brief. A title that says it all in three or four words scores highly.

Remember what Hamlet said when Polonius asked what he was reading: 'Words, words, mere words'.

What a damning answer!

Summarise, in your mind, what the chapter is to cover. Write it down, if you wish. Make sure you have overlooked nothing. Now start economising with words in your title. Aim for five or less. When you have cut it as far as you can, check that it still achieves its purpose. If you have any doubts, assume you have gone too far. Draw back to a reliable formula.

I really must keep it short

I must keep it short

Keep it short

Keep short

That's too short

Keep it short?

OK

Fig. 7. Choosing a chapter title.

Being informative

The titles to your chapters should tell the readers what the chapters deal with. They should help readers to find what they are looking for, without looking at the index.

Several years ago, a food processor advertised the reliability of his products with the slogan, 'What is named on the label is found in the jar'. You could do worse than adopt that principle. Abandon any waggish title that fails to measure up to it.

Attracting the maybe reader

When somebody who wants a book on your subject thumbs through what is on offer in the local bookshop, your book must sell itself. It must persuade the searcher that yours is the book to buy. Bear this in mind, all the time. The shopkeeper needs your help, as well as the publisher's. How you plan and present what you have to say will affect how well your book sells. The wording of your chapter headings is part of your presentation. If it says, 'Welcome', it may also say, 'Buy me'.

DIVIDING CHAPTERS INTO SECTIONS

Those non-fiction books that are **biographical** (whether in relation to an individual or to a group, a club, a society or a corporate enterprise) tell a story. They may retain the reader's interest by the suspense of wondering what is going to happen next and how the story will eventually end. And although the author of an autobiography must clearly have been alive when it was written, wondering what terror will come next may keep the reader on the edge of his or her seat. Anybody who has read Terry Waite's account of his years as a hostage can confirm this.

Non-fiction books with no biographical of quasi-biographical content lack that stimulus. (You know how boring a motorway can be, when there is a long distance between access points.) Authors of such books may be wise to adopt various devices to hold their readers' attention. Dividing sections – particularly long sections – into sub-sections is one of them. It is a useful practice, quite apart from its value in retaining attention. Each sub-heading separates what follows from what came before. In this way it:

● clarifies the text

● alerts the reader to a minor change of subject

● helps the reader to find a particular part of the subject, later.

LISTING APPENDICES

Many authors supplement the text of their non-fiction books with one or more appendices. They contain data that either would not sit comfortably in the text generally or is likely to appeal to a limited part only of the expected readership.

Useful addresses
This heading probably appears in more lists of appendices than any other. There are so many kinds of address that a reader may find helpful.

A teenager thinking about choosing a career borrows a book about many professions. It may include an appendix containing addresses where one can obtain details of the qualifications that are required for entry to each profession. It may also give details of training facilities that are available.

An older person, nearing retirement, has difficulty with understanding the employer's pension scheme. A book in the local library may explain, in simple language, what the scheme provides. It suggests to the reader that he or she may be entitled to more than the employer says. An appendix to the book gives an address to which the employee should send details of the situation and ask for expert advice.

Clearly an appendix that contains such useful addresses and many others adds greatly to the value of the book.

Glossary

Collins English Dictionary defines 'glossary' as 'an alphabetical list of terms, peculiar to a field of knowledge, with definitions or explanations'. When a book adds a glossary as an appendix, this defines or explains unusual words or phrases found elsewhere in the book. It may also include items of jargon that relate to the subject of the book, but do not appear elsewhere in it.

The first time a jargon word does appear in a book, the author should explain its meaning, in spite of its being given in the glossary. If readers have forgotten the meaning, when next they encounter the jargon, they will need to consult the glossary.

Recommending other books

A subject may be so vast that no single book covers more than a small part of what is known about it. An author who writes about one aspect or sector of the subject is not competing with writers who have tackled other areas. In effect they are an unknit team of collaborators. The author may encourage the readers of his books to explore further afield if he quotes details of the books of those other writers in the appendix.

Some of those books may no longer be in print. But searchers who try hard enough will probably discover where they can read them, even if they cannot buy or borrow them.

There is another kind of appendix that lists 'other books'. Their titles are all currently available. Your publisher is offering them to your readers because they may be interested in buying them. Doubtless your book will have similar publicity in other authors' books.

Identifying sources

Some authors use footnotes to identify sources of data. Others prefer to gather all the notes in one place, as an appendix, after inserting tiny reference numbers in the text.

The second system has the advantage of avoiding distracting readers' attention if they prefer to ignore the notes for most of the time. It retains the notes, for those who want them, but banishes them to a place where they are welcome to have all the space they need.

Acknowledgements

When a book contains pictorial illustrations, it is usual to acknowledge their origin, unless they came from the author or from the estate of the deceased subject of a biography. The credit may be given in the captions to the illustrations. Instead the origins may be listed in the contents page(s) at the beginning of the book or in an appendix.

Including charts and tables

For many purposes it is preferable to have charts and tables in or near the text to which they relate. They support what the author is saying. Relegating them to the back of the book may reduce their effectiveness. In other circumstances, an appendix is the right place for them.

In a history of the British Isles from 1066 to the present day, a table of key events during that period would provide the reader with a good overview if it was in an appendix. It would be out of place if it was somewhere in the text of one of the chapters.

Similarly, in a biography of a cricketer, tables of his achievements with bat and ball throughout his career come best at the end of the book. But an analysis of his figures for a particular match fits naturally into an account of that match.

CHECKLIST

● Have you grouped your material logically?

● Are your chapter headings brief and to the point?

● Will they attract somebody who is casually thumbing through the book?

● Are you dividing your chapters adequately into sections and subsections?

● Have you omitted any desirable appendices?

● Would any appendix material be better located in the main text of the book?

CASE STUDIES

Betty decides on her chapters

Having checked through the sorting of the pictures she has already taken, and added others that she plans to take, Betty sees no group that clamours to go first or last. She has given provisional titles to the chapters:

1. Did they mean it?
    Posters and other notices that might have been worded better

2. Friday afternoon jobs
    Accidental misspellings and other errors

3. Accidents will happen
    Spills and upsets

4. Undressed for the occasion
    Sartorial gaffes and disrobed misfortunes

5. A point of view
    You have to shoot it from the precise point

6. Not what I intended
    It happened as the shutter clicked.

Betty is confident that there will be sub-groups of illustrations within the chapters that will give scope for section headings.

She plans to add an introduction and a closing chapter. The former will explain that she believes that hilarity, like beauty, is in the eye of the beholder. The final chapter will contain suggestions for getting more fun from one's camera.

She also plans to include two appendices. The first will be a list of other books about photography. The second will be a glossary.

Charles plans his format

Charles returns to planning his book after completing the trek in four and a half months with Dick, his companion. They have tapes on which Charles noted details of their daily progress. Dick looked after the photography, using two cameras. In one he used black and white film to provide black and white illustrations. The other camera took colour transparencies. Dick wanted to be able to provide whatever illustrations the publisher preferred, when they were ready to approach one. They might also be able to sell an article to a glossy magazine, if they have good transparencies.

Charles proposes that the first two chapters of the book should be:

1. Why we went.

2. How we prepared.

Those would be followed by eight chapters describing the journey, the hazards and the points of interest along the route. Each chapter would relate to about 250 miles.

The final chapter would be 'What now?' There would probably be no appendices.

Margaret knows her readership

Margaret feels that she can cash in on the popularity of *Neighbours* and *Coronation Street* with millions of children in the UK. They know that the locations of these two soap operas are meant to be Melbourne and Manchester. She will contrast living in a vast conurbation, many miles from the sea, with living in a country where almost every major town was built on the coast.

Her provisional chapter headings are:

● Two hundred years young

● Arriving from many countries

● Farming the land

● Establishing financial services

● Developing mineral resources

● Coping with long distances

● Art and entertainment

● Ignoring the deserts.

Tony avoids the chronological approach

From his many sources of information, Tony has assembled a large amount of information about many aspects of the company's progress through 150 years. During those years, the accent has been on service to people. So he is delighted that much of his data has a human angle. He believes that he can bring this out better by devoting successive chapters to aspects of the company than by allotting 10 to 15 years to each chapter. The one exception would be the early years, when the company was establishing itself.

On this basis, he has chosen his chapter headings:

1. Friendly foundations
   The years when the company was a friendly society

2. The watchdogs
   Assessing the risks of insuring people's lives, and charging the right premiums

3. Keeping in step with the public
   Providing what people want

4. At the end of the day
   Paying out when a claim is made

5. Safeguarding the funds
   Investing the money safely yet profitably

6. Progress in persuasion
   Selling life assurance to those who need it

7. A base to work from
   Head office and branch office buildings

8. Under fire
   What happened to policy holders and staff in wartime

9. Men at the top
   CVs of some of the directors who have been on the board

10. The professionals
    Actuaries, medical offices, solicitors and accountants

11. The family which is the company
    When board, management and staff meet – on business or socially

12. Part of a wider community
    Relations with other insurance companies and local communities.

DISCUSSION POINTS

1. Should you include headings for sections and sub-sections in the synopsis?

2. How does one know if a word is jargon or not?

4
Finding a Publisher

Pessimism is the enemy of progress, but you need realism, as well as optimism, when you are an author. Before you go any further with your project, make sure that it is 90 per cent certain that somebody is going to publish it once you have written it. Writing your book first, and then looking for a publisher could end up with your phoning the Samaritans.

EXPLORING THE MARKET

At first glance you might think that you have already read all about this in Chapter 1. That is partly true. But you were then concerned with finding out what books there were already in circulation. Now you want to know:

- Are there publishers who would take on a book about my subject *now*?

- Which publishers are they?

- Would any of them publish *my* book?

- Which ones?

The notes you made at the outset, when you were locating existing books, may help. Who published them, especially the most recent books? (Times change, and publishers may change their priorities.) Do your notes give any clue to whether a publisher already regularly publishes work by one of your competitors? If so, that author may be well entrenched, leaving you little scope for a welcome from the publisher.

Seeing newspaper advertisements

You may be asking, 'Why do I have to explore the market, when some publishers are advertising for manuscripts in national newspapers?'

To comply with their advertisements, you would first have to write the whole book. You have already read that you could be wasting your time, if you did that without having a contract. Worse still, there are people who cater for what is referred to as 'vanity publishing'. This is a system where the author foots the bill for printing and marketing the book, and hopes to recover his outlay by selling all the copies. Why risk wasting your time and money, if you have made no attempt to have the book published in the generally approved way?

Looking more widely

Few, if any, types of book rely on one publishing house for their existence. *The Writer's Handbook* contains details of about 400 UK publishers. If you browsed through a copy in the reference department of your local library, you could glean some useful information. The book lists:

- names and addresses
- telephone and fax numbers
- how long a publisher has been in existence
- types of book published
- frequency of royalty payments
- sundry additional information.

Make a note of any publishers that look as if they might be interested. It will be useful in the next stage of your search. That will be when you go to the largest general bookshop you can visit.

When you did your earlier research in a shop you were looking specifically for books about your subject. Now you need to think more broadly. The publisher you are seeking may never have handled a book about your subject but be interested in something not too far removed from it. For example, if you have planned a book about investing one's savings, a publisher with titles about earning in your spare time might reasonably be interested.

Look for the shelves in the bookshop that come closest to your subject. Scan the titles for anything hopeful, especially if the publisher is one you noted as a possible from *The Writer's Handbook*. Look inside the books whose titles encourage you. If you have not already ticked them from your perusal of *The Writer's Handbook*, add them to your list, with other relevant details from the handbook.

CHOOSING NUMBER ONE

From all the publishers you have picked out as possibles, during your search, you must choose where to offer the book you aim to write.

Does anything you have discovered give you a gut feeling about this? If not, you need to work through what you know about each of the possibles. You might ask yourself a set of questions about each publisher:

● How does the normal format compare with my conception of my book?

● How near is my subject to the publisher's other recent books?

● How conveniently could I visit the publisher?

● Do I know anybody with experience of this publisher?

Avoid giving too much emphasis to the answer to any of those questions. If you live in Windermere, and the only factor that worries you about the publisher you would otherwise prefer is that the address is Worthing, ignore the fact. You will probably communicate only by letter or phone call. If all your efforts to make a wise choice achieve nothing, tossing a coin or using a pin may be your best bet, in the last resort.

MAKING A PROPOSITION

You want somebody to publish your book and sell it to prospective readers. First you must sell the project to a publishing house. Until one buys it, you are stuck. You have already pictured your reader. Now you must picture your publisher.

What the publisher wants

We all have rules we expect other people to follow. If they go their own way, instead, they lose brownie points with us. Many of us also have foibles – little preferences that we like to see people going along with. Try to find out what your chosen publisher's rules and foibles are.

You may know somebody who has had work accepted by the publisher. That would be a bonus. Have a word with him or her. You might be able to borrow a copy of the publisher's style sheet and use it as a basis for the way you present your proposition.

Without that stroke of luck, you need to create your own impression of the style you should adopt. Look more closely at some of the publisher's books in a bookshop. Their subjects may be very different from yours. That does not matter. Look at the contents pages at the beginning of the books:

● Is there a pattern about the way the chapter headings are worded?

● Is there a similarity about the number of chapters in the books?

● Do the appendices follow a pattern?

● Do they all have/lack a foreword?

If you pay the publisher the compliment of respecting any rules or foibles your questioning and searching reveals, you deserve any encouraging response it gains for you.

Presenting your synopsis

The contents pages in the publisher's books probably give you examples of acceptable layouts for a synopsis. They may list chapter headings only: they may also list section headings within the chapters.

Before going any further, look at the types of chapter headings used. Some publishers favour a particular style. Figure 8 gives various examples. If one of them resembles what you have seen in several of your target publisher's books, adopting it in your synopsis might improve your prospects.

When looking at your synopsis, the publisher may be satisfied that chapter headings provide enough detail to permit an assessment of the shape and suitability of your project. Or they may, at least, be enough to show whether it is a possible candidate for selection or a definite no-hoper. A brief letter from the publisher, asking you for further information, is likely to enable you to remove any doubts.

Growing Flowers

A life at sea

STALEMATE

All In It together

The Freelance Market

How can I improve my carpentry?

Matters of Life and Death

Planning Ahead

Learn to Sketch

Going away

A Penny For Them

Fig. 8. Examples of chapter headings.

Writing a supporting letter

You should not send your synopsis unaccompanied into the publisher's office. Back it up with a letter that gives it a purpose and a theme.

You must convince the publisher not only that somebody should write this book but also that you are that somebody. At this stage, you are the only person who believes that this is true.

Opening and closing

You are going to write a business letter to somebody you do not know. Even if you know the name of the person to whom you are addressing the letter, use a normal business mode of address, such as 'Dear Sirs', 'Dear Mr Brown' or 'Dear Miss Jones'. And close the letter with 'Yours faithfully' or 'Yours truly'. Wait for the publisher to take any steps towards a less formal style.

Matters to mention

● the subject of the proposed book

● target readers

- your relevant qualifications

- your experience as a writer

- any influence you have to promote sales of the book

- the likely length of the book

- the maximum time you would need to write the book

- if appropriate, the name of a recognised person who would write a foreword.

Keeping it short
Although you may have eight items to mention, you must keep your letter short and to the point. You are giving a stranger a specimen of your work. Avoid waffle.

And be positive. If you have no relevant qualifications or influence, make no mention of those matters.

Typing and sending your synopsis
It is, of course, assumed that both your synopsis and the covering letter will be typed on one side of good quality paper, preferably A4 size. They should be posted either flat or folded not more than once, and a stamped and addressed envelope for the publisher's reply should be enclosed.

REACTING TO NON-ACCEPTANCE

Every publishing house receives far more propositions than it can publish. Some stand out immediately as not meriting publication. Others are outside the areas that the target publishers deal with. And there are those that would be accepted if the publishers were not already handling as large a volume of work as they can cope with.

Whatever the reason for rejecting a proposition may be, publishers do not usually send rejection slips, such as editors of magazines use. They send a note, thanking you, regretting the decision and wishing you better luck elsewhere.

So if your proposition bounces, you should not lose heart. Try to look at it afresh. You may see it differently from the way you saw it when last you went through it.

Getting second opinions

A kind and valued friend may volunteer to read through your papers and try to make helpful suggestions. If you take up the kind offer and your friend checks through everything and expresses surprise that your work was turned down, keep calm. Bear in mind that your friend is not backing that judgement with cash. A publisher who accepted the task of turning your typescript into a book and selling it would lose the money he had invested in the book if it failed to sell.

However, if you know somebody who is in the world of professional writing, he or she may be able to make some helpful suggestions. Before asking for advice, make it clear that you are not looking for compliments. You genuinely want practical advice.

Trying again

After making any changes that you or a competent adviser thinks are desirable, look at your notes again and decide which publisher to target with your proposition, for your second attempt.

Go through the drill as if it was your first attempt. Group Captain Leonard Cheshire VC, said that he attributed his surviving 100 missions over enemy territory in World War 2, largely to his always preparing as carefully for each sortie as he did for his first.

If your synopsis is at all dog-eared or dirty, type it out again. A dog-eared synopsis carries its own death warrant.

Calling a halt

Publishers' letters, returning unwanted synopses, do not say, 'Frankly, I think you ought to throw it away and take up knitting'. They may say that your idea would not fit into their list. That could mean that the subject does not interest them, or they already have something about it in the pipeline.

What they would not do is make a response that you might interpret as an opening for you to write to them again or phone them. They have work to do.

How is one to know when one should stop sending one's idea to other publishers? There is no simple rule. One must use one's own judgement.

RESPONDING TO AN INTERESTED PUBLISHER

The flood of new books that reaches the shelves of bookshops, each year, proves that publishers accept some of the propositions they receive. So you may have grounds for hoping that your book will become part of the flood, if and when you contact the right publisher.

How will you find out? Your first intimation will probably be a letter from the publisher, acknowledging your letter, asking for more information and enclosing a **special CV form** for you to complete. The letter may also enclose a set of notes on the **house style** and ask you to send a specimen chapter of the book. Figure 9 outlines some of the material and information you may be asked to provide.

The special CV form will ask for your name, address, telephone number, and date of birth. It will also ask questions about your academic and occupational education and qualifications, and any instructional activities you have. Clearly the purpose is to assess your background not only for writing ability but also for attracting purchasers of the book. A good lecturer may have a captive market. You will see that it is in your interests to answer the questions as fully as possible.

When you are preparing the specimen chapter it would make sense for you to accustom yourself to the publisher's house style. The practice will be useful when the time comes for you to write the rest of the book.

Awaiting approval

After complying with the requirements of the publisher's letter, you may feel confident that you will soon receive the thumbs up sign. If so, you may decide to press on with writing the other chapters of your book. This will help to keep the design of the book fresh in your mind and to speed completion when you have the go ahead.

All being well, that should arrive in a few weeks, at most. When it comes, it will be in the shape of a **form of agreement** (or contract) between you and the publisher.

NOTING CONTRACT TERMS

The publisher prepares two copies of the form of agreement, each of which requires to be signed by both the author and the publisher. Each of the parties then retains one copy. It is a common practice for the publisher to sign both copies before sending them the the author, requesting him or her to sign both copies and return one of them to the publisher.

Before putting pen to paper, you should read the document and note all the provisions. They set out your rights and duties, and those of the publisher. Once you have signed both copies and the publisher has received one copy back, **the provisions are binding on both parties**.

In essence, the document:

● requires you to send the script of the book, of a given length, to the publisher by a given date

● requires the publisher to publish the book within a given period

● requires you to correct the proofs of the book within a given period of receiving them

● requires the publisher to make payments to you in respect of sales of the book or of rights relating to it, on given bases.

Those few lines give you the gist of what these documents usually contain, but you should read the whole of any document a publisher sends you. **Make sure you understand every part of it**. It is so easy to rush your fences when you are elated at having had an offer from a publisher for the first time. Figure 10 will give you an idea of the sort of terms you should expect to find in an authors' agreement form.

CHECKLIST

● When did this publisher last market a book on your subject?

● Which other publishers handle books on your subject?

● Is your synopsis in the publisher's particular style?

● Does your draft covering letter tell the publisher briefly what he will want to know about you and the book?

● Have you reviewed your synopsis and letter before trying another publisher?

● Have you given all the extra information the publisher asked for?

● Have you read the form of agreement, slowly and thoughtfully, before signing it?

1. **Author form** – which will request some of the following details:

   - name, address and date of birth
   - professional experience
   - articles or books published
   - radio/TV broadcasting experience
   - teaching experience
   - courses attended

2. **Structured book proposal** – may include:

   - title phrase
   - chapter headings
   - list of competing titles
   - blurb (see page 85)
   - list of possible illustrations

3. **Sample chapter** – if you are asked to supply a sample chapter all copy must be typed, and double spaced on A4 sheets, with generous left and right margins. Publishers will be looking for evidence that their standard features, *eg* bullet points, case studies and discussion points have been followed.

   Notes on house style – most publishers like their books to conform to basic conventions with regard to *eg*:

   - *ise* or *ize* spellings
   - punctuation
   - headings
   - presentation of figures.

Fig. 9. Example of information and material required by the publisher.

Information included in your author agreement

- name of the author
- title of the work
- approximate number of words
- date for delivery of typescript

Examples of some of the terms which will appear in your contract

1. It is the author's responsibility to obtain permission for the use of any copyright material.
2. The author is required to warrant to the publisher that the work is original and is not in violation of any existing copyright.
3. The author is required to warrant to the publisher that the work contains nothing indecent or libellous.
4. The author is required to read, check, correct and return proofs within a given period.
5. Copyright will be granted to the publisher or reserved by the author.
6. Copyright notice on every copy of the work shall include the name of the author.
7. The publisher is required to publish the book within a given period.
8. The publisher is required to pay an agreed royalty rate.
9. The publisher specifies an annual date for rendering a detailed account of the work.
10. The author has the right to examine the publisher's accounts in relation to the author's work.
11. The publisher shall be entitled after a given period following first publication to sell any surplus stock as a remainder.
12. Termination clauses will be included – *eg* if the author fails to present the work to the publishers by the agreed date or if the publisher fails to fulfil or comply with any of the provisions of the agreement, or goes into liquidation.

Fig. 10. Example of terms included in an author's agreement.

CASE STUDIES

Betty finds a publisher

Betty has searched through the details of all the publishers listed in *The Writer's Handbook* and picked out one that she believes will see the possibilities of her theme. She decides to vary slightly the formula for making a proposition, omitting section headings from her synopsis but including a draft chapter, with photographic illustrations, in colour.

Her chapter headings are:

1. Enjoying the ridiculous

2. Did they mean it?

3. Friday afternoon jobs

4. Accidents will happen

5. Undressed for the occasion

6. A point of view

7. Not what I intended

8. An eye for the odd

9. Planning the unexpected.

Betty explains, in her covering letter, that Chapter 1 will be an introduction, and Chapters 8 and 9 will make suggestions to help readers compile their own collections of ridiculous snaps.

Having studied the letter and synopsis, the publisher phones Betty and invites her to come to his office, with the whole collection of illustrations, so that he may consider her idea further. Their meeting and discussion of the proposition leads to Betty's being offered a contract to write and illustrate the book.

Charles sets himself a deadline

Charles and Dick have looked at books written by other travellers and chosen which to approach first. Charles prepares a synopsis for the book:

Beating Our Homeland's Bounds

List of illustrations
Preface

Charles has also approached the chairman of the charity to which he and Dick donated the sponsorship money they raised on their walk, and arranged that he will contribute a foreword to the book. Charles mentioned this in his letter to the publisher, after explaining why he and Dick had made the walk. He also says that they have a large selection of photographs, both prints and colour transparencies, to illustrate the book. He thinks that the book would be about 30,000-40,000 words long and would take about four months to write. (He admits that this is his first attempt at writing a book.)

After three weeks, Charles receives a letter from the publisher, inviting him to write Chapter 3, as a specimen for consideration. Charles writes the chapter but finds that it takes longer than he had expected.

The publisher phones Charles, says he likes the chapter but wonders if the approach of the beginning of the academic year will interfere with the writing of the book.

Charles says he has already written the first two chapters, in addition to the one the publisher has received, and is confident he can finish the job in time.

The publisher says he will put the form of agreement in the post, at once.

Margaret keeps persevering

Margaret tries to guess whether a publisher of travel books or school books would be more likely to find her proposition attractive. While unsure to which to send it, she drafts a fuller synopsis:

Australia – Land of Contrasts

List of illustrations

Preface

1. Two hundred years young
   Discovery
   Early exploration
   Penal colony
   People of imagination

2. Arriving from many countries
   The mother country
   Other Europeans
   From the New World
   Wider catchment

3. Farming the land
   Building the homesteads
   The Outback
   First generation offspring

4. Establishing financial services
   Banking
   Insurance
   Overseas trade

5. Developing mineral resources
   Importing machinery
   Mining coal and iron
   Iron and steel foundries
   Factories

6. Covering long distances
   Horse transport
   Sailing ships
   Railways
   Steamships
   Lorries and motor cars
   Aircraft

7. Art and entertainment
   Expanding townships
   Sport

Concerts and theatres
International sports people and entertainers

8. Ignoring the deserts
   Learning from experience
   Developing the hospitable land

Further reading

Glossary

Margaret sends the synopsis to a publisher who specialises in school books. In a covering letter she explains that she teaches geography to teenagers. She enlivens her classes by relating the places she talks about to what she saw and heard during visits she has paid to the areas. She finds that her pupils appreciate this. She would like to help children in other schools by books in which they can read what she would tell them if she was their teacher.

She would need six months in which to write this book, and it would be about 30,000 words long.

One of the publisher's editorial directors returns the synopsis, about a month later, regretting that she feels 'it is not suitable for our list'. Margaret revamps her covering letter, to send the synopsis to a publisher that specialises in travel books. After two more disappointments, she contracts to write the book for another travel book publisher.

Tony takes advice

Tony is in the privileged position of being virtually certain that his employers will pay to have his book published. However, the company's general manager arranges for a friend with publishing experience to vet the synopsis, and to offer suggestions about improving the text, in due course.

DISCUSSION POINTS

1. How would you set about finding a publisher?

2. How much of your book would you send to your chosen publisher?

3. What helpful comments would you hope to receive from a publisher who declined to publish your book?

4. Would it be a good idea to ask a friend to comment on your book, before sending it to a publisher?

5
Drafting Your Book

At last you can get down to the nitty gritty. You can feel confident that all the work you have done so far has not been wasted.

SORTING MATERIAL

You probably have a mass of material that you have been accumulating since you embarked on this project. Some of it may be notes jotted down as you refreshed your memory on parts of the subject that you rarely thought about. Other notes may relate to recent changes and developments. Whatever the details are, you need to sort them into order.

Modern typing and word processing equipment offer an author great scope for moving chunks of text from one place to another. But life is far simpler if one starts with the right sequences of facts and ideas.

Choosing the right sequence

What is the right sequence? The answer to that question may not be obvious. It may not be the way you look at it, from the viewpoint of your months or years of experience. The right sequence is the one that will be easiest for a novice to understand. The novice is the reader whom you were picturing at the beginning of Chapter 2, when you were planning the scope of the book.

Try to put yourself in that person's place. Can you remember your first approach to the subject, many years ago? It may have been when you had recently left school or further education. Or perhaps you had just made a mid-life job change, or suffered a marital breakdown or bereavement. Whenever it was, does it have any bearing on your subject? Make good use of your own memories and those of other people you know.

SEIZING THE READER'S INTEREST

You need to grab your reader's attention. How are going to do that?

'"Heaven helps those who help themselves" is a well-tried maxim.' An author opened the first chapter of a non fiction book with those words. It sold a quarter of a million copies. His name was Samuel Smiles and the title of the book was *Self-Help*. It was first published in 1859. Penguin Books published it again, in paperback, in 1986.

That maxim is still current today, but not as well known as it was, even 50 years ago. Here are two more recent examples of diving into a subject.

'When families and tribes wandered round the world with their flocks or created tribal settlements to live in, nobody needed a pension scheme.' Those are the opening words in a book about modern pensions written in 1982.

'Retirement can be the most exciting adventure in the whole of life.' A book about preparing for retirement started like that, in 1987.

In each of those books, the first sentence mentioned the subject of the book, but not as the reader might have expected. Greet your reader with a sentence that hits the target from an unexpected angle.

Holding your reader's attention

Have you ever been the first speaker after lunch at a seminar? If you have, you know that members of your captive audience tend to nod off. That can happen to your readers when they have devoured a few paragraphs or pages of your book. A novelist faces the same problem, and deals with it by posing a new problem for the main character as soon as the latest crisis is on the verge of being resolved. You need to achieve something similar, to keep your reader aware of what you are saying.

A change of typeface, the insertion of a diagram or questionnaire, or an offbeat remark could snatch back the wanderer's attention. Keep your reader on the alert.

BEING SIMPLE AND PRECISE

'I hear you were quite a hit on that training day last week,' the general manager said. 'Congratulations!'

'Thank you, sir. They made it easy for me. They asked me if I could put the new rules in simple language, and I did just that.'

1. Take a typical sample of what you have written, about 100 words long. (It must start at the beginning of a sentence and finish at the end of a sentence.)

2. Count the exact number of words and divide by the number of sentences.*

3. Count the number of words with three ** or more syllables and add this to the average number of words in a sentence.

4. Multiply the answer by 0.4 to obtain the fog index.

Gunning would expect a passage with an index of 4 to be intelligible to an 11 year old, and an index of 8 to a 14 year old. For an index of 12 he would need a sixth-former: an index of 16 he would feel unsuitable for a reader in less than higher education. He condemned all passages with an index of more than 18.

* A sentence divided by a colon or semi-colon counts as two sentences if a full stop could replace the other punctuation mark.

** Words with three syllables, merely because they end with -es or -ed may be ignored. So may words like school-teacher, that are made from two words, and proper names.

For example, 'Elizabeth and Jonathan nearly drowned at sea: they were surfboarding,' would count as two sentences, totalling ten words.

Fig. 11. Fog index (invented by American business teacher, Robert Gunning).

'I should have said that was quite an achievement. Plenty of people can make simple things complicated. Very few can make complicated things simple.'

The GM was right. You will always do your readers a favour if you try to keep things simple. Where should you start?

Oliver Goldsmith wrote a poem called 'The Deserted Village'. In it he said of the village schoolmaster that his:

> 'Words of learned length and thund'ring sound
> Amazed the gazing rustics rang'd around'.

Cut out the learned length and thund'ring sound! The amazement will disappear. Multisyllabic pomposity is out of place in the kind of book you are writing, unless you are using it facetiously. It is usually showing off. Use short words in short sentences, and short paragraphs. They can work marvels for making things clear. From time to time try using the **fog index**, described in Figure 11, to check on one aspect of your simple writing.

Avoiding ambiguity

There is more than brevity of word and sentence to simple writing. The words need to be adequate and in the right order, too. Take the sentence, 'Coming into the room, I saw Henry's mother'. It has brevity, but is the meaning clear? Was it I or Henry's mother who was coming into the room? In other words, should the sentence be, 'As I was coming into the room, I saw Henry's mother' or 'I saw Henry's mother coming into the room'?

That may seem like the kind of example schoolteachers give to teenagers in English lessons, but older and more experienced people can create the same problems. A poster that appeared on hoardings in 1996 said, 'Smoking while pregnant can harm your baby's health'. Surely no baby should be either smoking or pregnant, let alone both. To create a slogan with punch, the copywriter jettisoned 'you are' from the expression 'while you are pregnant', leaving 'your baby' as the only person to be smoking and pregnant. (This may be even clearer in the briefer version shown in Figure 12.) The slogans doubtless raise few eyebrows among the people who see them. But you need to write for your readers in a way that avoids ambiguity.

Using active verbs

'Use verbs in preference to nouns, and active verbs in preference to passive verbs.' That is a maxim every author needs to bear in mind. In reinforces the text. It turns pious hopes into actions.

Fig. 12. A very precocious baby!

● The opening time for this branch of the bank is 9.30.

● This branch of the bank will open at 9.30.

● The Assistant Manager will open this branch of the bank at 9.30.

Compare the impact of those three sentences. The first makes a statement. The second makes a promise. The third is by far the strongest. It is precise. It lays the blame at the Assistant Manager's door if he or she fails to open the door on time.

AVOIDING JARGON

If you are a computer buff writing a book for computer buffs, by all means use computer jargon. If your book is for people who are struggling to learn to use a personal word processor for writing to their friends, try to use language that lay people understand.

There may be times when you feel that life would be easier for your readers and for you if you introduced some jargon. For example, Chapter 4 mentioned that publishers have preferences about the language authors use and the way they present their work. The jargon expression for a publisher's preferences is 'house style'. It has nothing to do with the architecture of the building where the publisher's office is.

If you want to use a jargon word or phrase in your book, explain it the first time you use it. Include it in the glossary, too, for the benefit of any readers who forget the definition.

USING VIVID LANGUAGE

A touch of imagination in the words you use can help to hold the readers' attention and impress what you are saying on their minds. The American journalist who write of her subject, 'She was infanticipating,' scored better on the impact scale than she would have done with, 'She was pregnant'.

Sir Winston Churchill was a master of the eloquent phrase or sentence:

'These are not dark days: these are great days – the greatest days our country has ever lived.'

'I have nothing to offer but blood, toil, tears and sweat.'
'We are waiting for the long-promised invasion. So are the fishes.'
'Give us the tools, and we will finish the job.'

All those words are simple, but they breathed defiance and rallied the nation.

You may not have Churchill's flair for the phrase that super-charges simple words: you can still extract 50 per cent extra effect from them, if you give them a little thought.

If you had written, 'Napoleon lived in exile for less than six years after his defeat at Waterloo,' you might inject more pathos by changing it to, 'Death in agony ended Napoleon's life less than six years after Wellington had shattered the Frenchman's career'.

PROVIDING ILLUSTRATIONS

'"What is the use of a book," thought Alice, "without pictures or conversation?"' Today's children echo that quotation from *Alice in Wonderland*. The sale of glossy magazines shows that adults appreciate pictures, too. And publishers of paperback biographies include one or more sections of pictures to boost their sales.

The subjects of some non-fiction books do not lend themselves to the inclusion of pictures. In spite of this, many books benefit by using **illustrations** of a different kind. Graphs, tables, diagrams and questionnaires are all illustrations. So are words and figures that show how principles apply in practice. The case studies in this book show you one way of using word pictures.

If you use several examples of how quotations for a service are calculated, be careful to relate them to men and women, married and unmarried, of widely differing ages and occupations, if possible.

Take time to consider what kind of illustrations would most enhance your book. It might benefit from the inclusion of more than one kind. Bear that in mind when you are glancing back through each chapter.

PREPARING APPENDICES

You may lighten your task considerably if you keep your eyes and ears open and jot down in your notebook any odd item you come across that you think could fit into an appendix. If you start the notebook when you are looking at the market, you should have a handy nucleus when the time comes for you to draft the appendices.

Compiling the glossary

While you are writing your book, list any words or phrases that you think should be included in the glossary.

When the time comes to compile it, refrain from lifting a glossary, ready made, from somebody else's book. If you did that, it could be said that you were stealing. On the other hand, it would be reasonable to compare a list of words you were proposing to define with lists in other books. You might add to your list any word or phrase you had missed, but it would be wrong for you to copy the definition.

Make your definitions as short and simple as you can. If you have any doubt about a meaning, check it with a dictionary, but do not adopt the dictionary definition. Your entry must be your own work.

If you use a jargon word in a definition, make sure that your glossary contains a definition of that word.

Listing useful addresses

List the addresses and phone numbers of organisations that you know to be useful for your readers.

Add any other organisations, said to be similarly useful, that you have gleaned from newspapers, magazines or other books. Check the addresses and phone numbers by phoning the organisations. Do not rely on directories *etc.* They become out-of-date.

Check the purposes of the organisations from their latest yearbooks or comparable sources. If you have no such reliable information, write to the organisations, asking for a statement you could publish in your book. They will usually be glad of the publicity.

Suggesting further reading

What you include under this heading must depend on your own judgement. This will take into account the nature of the subject. If you have been studying other books and distilling their knowledge, you may be happy to list them, for the benefit of readers who wish to study the subject more deeply.

In general you will not want to give publicity to competitors.

Your publisher will probably be pleased to advertise other books from the house's current list.

Writing the preface

It may appear strange to include a paragraph about the preface near the end of this chapter. Experience suggests that writing it is best left until you have written the remainder of the book. You can then include any warnings you need to give to readers about how the book deals with various matters. You can also include a few words of appreciation for people who have helped you by commenting on the script or assisting with the typing.

It is much easier to forecast what the book will contain, with hindsight.

CHECKLIST

● Have you used the fog index?

● Are you being precise?

● Have you used jargon unnecessarily?

● Are you putting punch and zest into what you are writing?

● Have you used adequate and appropriate illustrations?

CASE STUDIES

Betty strikes the right note

Betty adopts a friendly, conversational style in her first chapter. She chats her way through examples of what makes some people laugh but leaves others unmoved.

She first quotes the Munchhausen story of the tired horseman in a desolate, snow-covered landscape who tethers his mount to a metal spike sticking up through the snow and lies down to sleep. He wakes up in a strange village, where he is surrounded by people looking up at a church steeple. From the top, a horse is hanging by its neck.

Betty apologises to those readers who find the impossible gargantuan thaw, that is the basis of the story, stupid and unfunny. Her book is not for them.

The next six chapters contain the six groups of photographs that inspired her to write the book. Alongside or beneath each picture she wants the publisher to print a note of where and when she took the photograph, and what appealed to her about it. She has written all the captions for the pictures. She is confident that, in each case, the humour of the caption matches that of the picture.

In Chapter 8 she demonstrates how she found various situations and tampered with them to produce comical results. For some of them, a series of pictures accompanies the narrative.

In Chapter 9 Betty describes how she dreamed up some potentially amusing settings and used her imagination to predict where she might find the right locations for photographing them.

Having written in a light-hearted vein, she has not used words that require her to include a glossary. However, her last two chapters encourage her readers to use more imagination, so she prepares a list of other reading, including both books and magazines, that she believes some readers could find helpful.

Charles meets his deadline

Preparing Chapter 3 as a specimen for the publisher, Charles finds that he can write more speedily than he had thought likely.

Dick has helped by checking each chapter as Charles has finished writing it. He has also picked out photographs to illustrate the chapters and prepared captions for them.

The chairman of the charity, too, has helped by skimming through the draft chapters and writing his foreword.

The work is ready for Charles to start his final revisions, a month before he is due to go to university.

Margaret gathers her material

Margaret writes to her friend in Australia, sending her a copy of the synopsis and asking her for handouts relating to as many of the chapters and sections as possible. She would also like to receive some pages of job vacancy advertisements covering a wide range of jobs.

While waiting for this material to arrive, Margaret visits her local library and borrows any books that have a bearing on her subject. She also locates all the holiday snaps she can find that were taken during either of her holidays in Australia.

She buys 1,000 index cards, 5" x 3", and starts to make notes on them of all the helpful facts she finds during her reading of the library books. She sorts them into groups to match the headings in the synopsis.

After six weeks, the first parcel arrives from Australia. An air letter has warned her that collecting the remaining items will delay a second parcel by about a fortnight. The waiting period is easily filled with writing notes on what Margaret has already received.

When the second parcel arrives, she:

● picks out the items in it that refer to her first chapter
● sorts all the note cards relating to that chapter into order
● starts writing.

Tony passes the committee test

With the suggestions made by the general manager's knowledgeable friend in front of him, Tony starts to write the book. He bears in mind the vast range of people who are going to receive copies of the book, and his determination that they should read it. To seize and retain their interest, he makes sure that a touch of humour or an unusual situation crops up at frequent intervals.

When the text is complete, Tony shows it first to the general manager's friend, who suggests some improvements. Having made them, Tony passes the text to the general manager, who approves it, apart from the final paragraph. He rewrites this, in a style totally different from Tony's.

Tony rewrites the paragraph, retaining all the points the GM wants to make but using language consistent with the remainder of the book. The GM approves and sets up a committee, chaired by himself and including Tony, a professional publisher and his designer. Tony roots out old photographs, colourful leaflets and posters from the company's archives. The publisher has the text of the book set up in the chosen typeface and obtains some useful illustrations from a photograph library. The designer combines the text and illustrations in a thoughtful layout and the committee approves it.

DISCUSSION POINTS

1. Should you keep looking back at what you have written, or delay correcting until you have finished the chapter?

2. Is there a danger that readers might think that humour implies that the author was not taking the subject seriously?

3. Does using jargon show that one is familiar with the subject?

4. Does vivid language include strong language?

6
Revising the Text

'The man who makes no mistakes does not usually make anything.'

A visiting American diplomat said that in a speech at the Mansion House, nearly 100 years ago. Successful authors will agree. They always need to revise the text when they reach the end of the first draft of a book. Not a lot, maybe, but they need to check what they have written and remove or correct the mistakes.

This chapter mentions several ways in which your revision of your work may improve it. When you come to apply them, keep your eyes open for all of them, all of the time. Resist the temptation to remedy an error as soon as you spot it. Wait until you have at least read the whole of the paragraph or section and checked whether there are other things that need attention. Unless you do this, you will find yourself needing to rewrite some sentences and paragraphs several times, for different reasons. Patience can save you valuable time.

> Patience is a virtue –
> Possess it, if you can –
> Found seldom in a woman
> And never in a man.

Before you start revising your first draft, make sure that you have two essential books beside you. One is an up-to-date dictionary; the other is a thesaurus. You need the first book to check both the meaning and the spelling of words. You need the second to supply a better word when what you have written fails to achieve the precise meaning you mean to convey, or to have adequate impact.

You may already have been referring to both of those books while making your first draft. Excellent! Keep up the good work.

REMOVING ERRORS

'Did I really write that? Good heavens!' you say. Yes, sometimes you may have a pleasant surprise when you reread something you wrote a while ago.

But sometimes you may reread a chapter you wrote last week, and wince with horror. Thank goodness you can delete or rewrite the bad bit before you send the draft to the publisher.

What shook you, when you read it, may be:

● a misstatement of the facts, as you knew them

● a misleading statement of the facts

● a statement that was true but has since become untrue.

If either of the first two situations applies, you need to rewrite your statement so as to give a true and fair view of the facts. In the third situation, you might be wise to write on such lines as, 'before 10 October 199X it was not lawful to . . . but since that date . . .'.

You must do your utmost to ensure that the book is accurate when it first appears in the bookshops. With this in mind, you should correct the text up to the time when it goes to the publisher. If a change occurs after that but before the book goes on sale, you should advise the publisher immediately so that a slip notifying the change may be put inside each copy of the book.

Checking spelling and meaning

Do you have any doubts about the spelling of a word you have used? You were happy with it when you wrote it, but now you are less certain. Check it with the dictionary. It is easy to slip up when a long time has elapsed since you last used the word. If there are alternative spellings given, make sure you always use the same one. And while you have the dictionary open, look at the definition. Maybe you guessed its meaning from the context, years ago, and have never checked that you were right. It would be a pity to lose credibility by misusing the word now.

Finding repetitions and contradictions

It is easy to be so intent on mentioning a point that one repeats it. There are times when a reminder of a vital fact that you mentioned 20 or 30 pages earlier may be desirable. That is fine. Make a point of emphasising it to your readers. Accidental double entries are different. Be alert to see them and delete them.

You may also find that you appear to be contradicting what you said in an earlier chapter. Stop and think about it. Are you disagreeing with yourself or is there a subtle difference between your two statements? If the former is true, you need to correct whichever statement is untrue. If there is a subtle difference between the versions, you need to clarify the position. It may be easy for readers to miss the subtlety.

You may be writing primarily for the model reader you visualised when you started planning your book. This is fair enough. But you should try to give their money's worth to all the other people who buy the book – including any who miss your subtleties.

ADDING ANYTHING OMITTED

If somebody writing a letter omits to include one item, it is not necessary to take a clean sheet of paper and start again. Instead, the writer may finish the letter, sign it, and add a postscript. Authors have no such easy way of dealing with the situation. They must find the place in the chapter where the additional material ought to go, and dovetail it in.

Often a more drastic rebuilding is needed. The finished article should look more like a purpose-built structure than a brick-built house with weatherboarding annexes.

Some of the additions you need to make are probably things you had intended to say but forgot. Others are those that you expected to omit, but later realised ought to go in. The book would be incomplete without both sets, plus the inspirations that have come to you while you have been writing the book.

The easiest omissions to deal with require no more disruption of the text than inserting a couple of extra sentences or paragraphs. Other additions call for major rewriting of sections or chapters of the book. The more drastic the remedy that is called for, the more important it becomes to deal with any other necessary alterations at the same time.

Adding illustrations

Are there any matters you have written about that would become clearer if you added an illustration of some kind? Now is the time to deal with them. That is especially true of narrative examples of how a process you have mentioned works out in practice. Making space for inserting pictures, diagrams or tables may cause less disruption than breaking into the text to include a 'for example'.

Creating striking openings

Do any of your chapters or sections lack effective openings? If they do, adding punch to them could give your book a lift.

How should you set about creating a phrase or sentence that will make the reader sit up and take notice? There is no golden rule. As Edison said of genius, writing a good opening sentence is 'one per cent inspiration and 99 per cent perspiration'.

Are there any practical tips for making good use of the perspiration? You might pick out the key word in the subject of the chapter or section and experiment with combining it with other relevant words, shuffling them around. Or you could look up the key word in a book of quotations or proverbs. That might provide either something you could quote as it stood or the germ of an idea for you to develop.

A couple of examples will illustrate this. If you were writing a chapter about CVs and wanted an opening sentence for a section headed 'Experience', you might find two quotations that included that word. Oscar Wilde wrote that it was 'the name that every one gives to their mistakes'. Dr Johnson said that a widower's speedy remarrying, after the death of his nagging wife, was 'the triumph of hope over experience'.

If you quoted Wilde, you might add that one hoped that the person reading the CV had not read Wilde's comment. If you preferred Johnson, you might misquote him by opening with, 'A good CV earns the triumph of experience over hope'.

SLIMMING THE TEXT

The French philosopher, Pascal, once wrote, 'I have made this letter longer than usual, only because I have not had the time to make it shorter'. The person to whom he was writing doubtless took the comment as an apology for having written in a hurry. One must assume that Pascal thought the situation demanded speed rather than polished prose.

An author may be in a hurry, too. He or she has a deadline to meet. But before accepting it, the author should have checked that the deadline allowed enough time for revising the text.

Letters usually relate to immediate matters. They soon end up in a file that is opened rarely or a wastepaper basket that is emptied frequently. Books usually have longer active lives than that.

And few letters are read by more than a handful of people, but most books have many readers. The time an author devotes to pruning surplus words benefits all those people, and is well spent.

Cutting out passenger words

How does one slim the text? First by deleting any of those phrases, in parenthesis, that have crept into so many people's speaking and writing. A common example is 'if you like'. It belies its appearance. It looks as if it invites the listener's or reader's indulgence, but it does no such thing. It does nothing.

The same can be said of the word 'basically'. Some people use it at the beginning of sentence after sentence that contain nothing basic. It follows in the footsteps of the word 'actually' that used to figure so largely in what many people said.

Then there are expressions that use several words where one would do, such as 'in this day and age', instead of 'now'. It may have carried emphasis, the first time somebody used it. It has become a cliché.

Less obvious examples of passenger words are the adverb 'very' and many adjectives. That apparently sweeping statement needs explaining. It is easy to add 'very' before an adjective that needs no emphasis. Doing this devalues 'very'. Its ultimate misuse is in 'very unique'. When something is unique, it stands alone: nothing duplicates it. So to describe it as 'very unique' or 'most unique' is nonsense. And references to a little dwarf or an elderly octogenarian contain superfluous adjectives.

> There was a young man of Japan
> Whose limericks never would scan;
> When they said it was so,
> He replied, 'Yes, I know,
> But I always try to get as many words into
>   the last line as ever I possibly can'.

Removing pet expressions

Unlike pet animals, pet expressions usually arrive without the owner's knowledge. Take the example of George's stock response to hearing something new. It has amused John for several months before he found an opportunity to tackle George about it, discreetly.

He said, 'George, may I ask you a personal question?'

'Of course you can, as long as it isn't an intimate one.'

'Thank you. Why is it that whenever somebody tells you something you didn't know, you say, "Really! Is that a fact?"?'

George replied, 'Really! Is that a fact?'

When John laughed, George asked, 'What's the joke?' He was totally unaware of what he had done. His response to John's question had been a reflex reaction.

You may not know what your pet phrases are. Keep alert, as you revise your text. Try to notice expressions that appear more than two or three times. When you find them:

- make a note of them
- remove them from the text
- put a warning sign on your desk.

BEWARE
PET EXPRESSION

Conscious pet expressions

Some people create their own expressions and repeat them *ad nauseam*. They tend to become boring to the listener or reader. A frequent source of these is spoonerisms that amused the perpetrator when he or she accidentally said 'nosey cook' instead of 'cosy nook', or 'fighting a liar' instead of 'lighting a fire'. The original incident may be hilarious: repetition of the words with the transposed first letters bores the reader.

That brilliant piece of prose

Perhaps the most important item to delete is the sentence you polished with such care. By the time you had finished with it, it shone. Churchill would have revelled in it – but it has lost its relevance. Ditch it. And stifle any urge to find somewhere else to use it.

POLISHING THE PRESENTATION

You planned to use simple language and short sentences when you started to write your book. How are you measuring up to that standard? It is easy to pile on the words as you try to make a point. Watch for long sentences as you revise the text. Where they have more than 20 words, try to divide them into shorter sentences. You might achieve that by rewording them.

● Sometimes switching the order of the parts of a sentence can do the trick. Try starting with the second half, and following it with the first half. The result may amaze you.

● Do any of the words sit uncomfortably with each other? Try using different words.

● Do any of the words look out of place with the subject matter? If they worry you, they may worry a reader, too. Replace them with something better, if you can.

● Look carefully at any sentence that fails to jell. Are you relying on a noun to carry it? Is the verb in the passive voice? Try rejigging it with an active verb.

● Never hesitate to rewrite a paragraph if it sags. Give the reader something that compels him to press on now and to wait impatiently for your next book.

DELETING WHAT MIGHT OFFEND

Mark Twain said, 'When people do not respect us, we are sharply offended.' If he was right, you should always respect your readers and let your respect shine through. They have earned it. They are reading your book.

Because you respect them, you will check that you write nothing that might offend them. That is sometimes more easily said than done. Occasionally a person takes offence at what seemed to be an innocuous remark. There may be a situation of which hardly anybody is aware but which makes the offended person unusually vulnerable. That is one of life's hazards. There is nothing you can do about it.

But you can avoid many of the potential ways of offending your readers. You can steer clear of making remarks that might upset anybody who holds strong views about politics or religion. Even if the purpose of your book is advertised as being an explanation of your views on one of those taboo topics, you can be polite. There is no need for you to imply that people who disagree with you are morons or mentally unbalanced.

The scope for ill-advised comment extends beyond the realm of personal beliefs. It is possible to appear supercilious in the way you write, just as in the way you speak. Bear that in mind. Think twice before you use an expression such as 'It is obvious that . . .'. It may be obvious to you and to the people you associate with in your work or your social life. If it will not be obvious to some of your readers, leave those words out.

CHECKLIST

● Are you satisfied that you are using the right words and spelling them correctly?

● Have you: – corrected all the errors?
– repaired all the omissions?
– removed everything superfluous?
– deleted everything potentially offensive?
– reworded everything obscure?
– satisfied yourself with the sequence?

CASE STUDIES

Betty revises her photographs
Betty rereads her first chapter slowly, searching for excessive wordage. She decides that there is little she can do to slim it down. The Munchhausen story illustrates her taste in humour so well.

She finds several captions that need improving in the next six chapters, and she goes out with her camera one weekend to take further shots of two subjects that she felt were poorly presented in the existing photographs.

She checks that none of the books or magazines she has listed as further reading has become out of print or ceased production.

Charles completes his revision
Thanks to the suggestions Dick has made after reading the whole of

the text, Charles finds that he is able to complete his revision of the text in a week, to the relief of the publisher.

Margaret uses her judgement

Before attempting to reread any of what she had written, Margaret thumbed slowly through her 1,000 cards to satisfy herself about the sequence. She made a couple of alterations, neither of which involved her in significant changes to the text. Following a hunch, she hung a Scenic Australia calendar on the wall behind her desk. She turns a page over, each day, so that she is constantly reminded of the great variety of scenery. She finds that it helps her to feel the country's atmosphere when she is working on the book.

She invited one of her colleagues to vet one of the chapters but quickly discovered that the lady wanted to rewrite the book, in her own style. So Margaret decided to rely on her own judgement – and a good dictionary – as her guide to revising the text.

Tony has little to revise

Owing to the circumstances in which he has been writing the book, revision of the text has been an ongoing process. There was little left for Tony to do, in this context, when he had complied with all the advice he had received.

DISCUSSION POINTS

1. Is your book now like 'the law of the Medes and Persians, which altereth not'?

2. Have you been ruthless enough with pet expressions?

7
Updating an Existing Book

'Let's give it a new lease of life', the sales director suggests. His travellers have told him that the book has started to date and booksellers have stopped reordering it.

The suggestion sounds like prescribing a remedy for a condition without having diagnosed it. The sales director may be proposing a shot in the arm when the ailing book needs a transplant.

'I had a word with the author last week', the editorial director says. 'He's drawing a pension now, and he's out of touch with the subject. He mentioned a woman who took over most of his work when he retired, and suggested she might be willing to update the book. I phoned her yesterday, and she promised to think about it and let me know if she would take it on.'

If you were in her position and agreed to accept the challenge, what would you do next?

NOTING WHAT CHANGES ARE NEEDED

Where should you start? The latest edition of the book must be one of the most likely places for anybody in that situation to choose. In any event, it would make sense for you to have at least one copy to work on, and read it. If you can have two copies, take them. You can mark all the out-of-date information with a highlighter pen in one copy. Keep the other in reserve. You may want it for another purpose, later. (If that other purpose crops up and you have no second copy, using a differently coloured highlighter may help.)

During the next ten days, check back on changes of law, market practice, manufacturing methods, examination syllabuses, people's tastes and any other relevant matters that have occurred since the date of the previous edition. What matters are relevant depends largely on the subject of the book. They may differ as widely as schooling and leisure interests. List all the changes. Background information will be valuable when you start writing.

When looking in the front of the book for the date of the previous edition, note also when other earlier editions were published. Try to borrow copies of them.

If you reread the book after a ten-day break, you may find other outdated information that you missed on the first reading. Highlight it, too.

SEEING WHERE CHANGES ARE NEEDED

Where does the book need revision, to take account of all the changes that ought to be made? The sidelining and other marks you have made in the previous edition give at least part of the answer. They may not cover everything. Some of the developments that have occurred may require a new chapter. Others may make an existing chapter obsolete.

The whole shape of the book may need rethinking. On the other hand, the addition of one or two chapters, at the end of the book, might achieve all that the situation requires. Think flexibly. There is no standard formula for doing this part of the work.

Keep an open mind. Until you have a comprehensive view of the task, it is too early to crystallise your ideas.

MATCHING OR CHANGING STYLE?

Gielgud's and Olivier's Hamlets may have differed markedly. A brilliant impressionist could imitate the portrayal by each so closely that a dedicated Shakespeare buff could not distinguish between the original and the copy.

Matching a style of authorship can be less difficult. Unlike the impressionist the wordsmith has an adequate specimen of the previous author's work at hand. It simplifies his version of invisible mending.

That does not mean that every author can patch any other author's work so neatly that a reader does not see the join. Many authors may lack the facility. They always use something near their own distinctive style.

Arguing for change

The decision whether to match or change the previous style should take account of more than the chosen author's flexibility of expression. The market may want a fresh approach. Salesmen may have heard comments such as, 'Not another one by Bloggins. Isn't he a bit past it?' or 'I did hope the book would have a new format this time'.

Looking back at the earlier editions of the book, you might find that much of the design and content of the last one dated back to the 1970s. Any such discovery should quickly end any debate as to whether to change the format but retain the old style of dust jacket, or keep the format but change the dust jacket.

Arguing against change

The publisher has the same objective as you. He wants the book written the way that will be the most profitable. Perhaps some salesmen have heard that Bloggins' retirement has saddened customers. They were looking forward to his next edition. So retaining his style, if not his authorship, might be wise.

Looking at earlier editions you might find that he had always updated his presentation when he updated the information in the book. Then following his practice could make sense.

PLANNING THE LAYOUT

You and the publisher may agree that it would be simplest and most effective for you to retain as much of the previous edition as possible. You will then need to write any new or amended passages in the previous author's style. But if much of the work is still his craftsmanship, any revision of the layout, other than what he would have made, would appear to be illogical.

On the other hand, you and the publisher might agree that you should use your own style, from start to finish. In that case, you could do worse than put the previous layout out of your mind. Try to forget the book, for a few days. Find something else to keep you busy. You might reread Chapter 3 of this book.

When you come back to your task, take a clean sheet of paper and try to create an original layout. After a couple of days, compare it with the previous one. Try to make an unbiased judgement. Look for the good and bad points in each. You may finish up with an amalgam of the two.

MAKING CHANGES

If you are creating a new book, the old one largely ceases to figure in your work. (You may still use it as one of the many sources of data for your book.)

This section of this chapter is concerned with your updating the existing book.

Allocating information

You have listed the information you need to bring in, or alter or remove. You need to allocate it to chapters and sections in the updated layout. If you are discontinuing any of the existing chapters you will need to allocate any residual parts of them to other chapters.

Before starting to alter the book, you need to allocate each item on your list to the place where it should appear in the book. To facilitate this, you could number each item and make a chart (see Figure 13). List the chapters and sections of the book in sequence down the side and provide space for entering the numbers of the items of information alongside the appropriate places.

Chapter	Section	Change number
1	Opening	4 7 11 20
1	Losses	3 15 45
etc	*etc*	*etc*

Fig. 13. Chart of necessary alterations.

It may be desirable to mention some items in more than one place. If so, you should list the items' numbers alongside each of the places in the chart.

If you cross through the relevant number on the chart, each time you deal with an item, the chart will provide a check on the completion of the changes in the text of the book.

Applying the information

Starting at the beginning of the first chapter, you must systematically work through the book, revising the text wherever you need to take account of an item on the list. The chart will warn you when such an alteration will be needed. It will not warn you when you are coming to a passage that needs to be improved. So while keeping an eye open for the precise place for a factual update, you need also to be alert to notice a word, a phrase or a sentence that warrants alteration. It may be out of fashion, unclear or awkward. It may suffer from at least two of these faults.

When you have made the alteration, the passage should:

● read well

● match the style of the rest of the book

● be accurate and clear

● give effect to any item on your chart that is involved.

Only when you have satisfied all these criteria should you cross out the number of the item on the chart and move on.

There may be many parts of the book where little of the text needs alteration. They offer a more relaxed period after the stress of mastering more complex passages, but they can encourage a reviser to speed up too much. After skimming through half a dozen pages that needed no attention, you may miss a sentence that you ought to clarify. Such lapses of concentration feature in many kinds of activity. When you find yourself in one of those drowsy periods:

● stop for half a minute, after every three or four pages

● look away from your work

● take a deep breath

● return to the job.

Choosing the facilities

What facilities are you going to have for altering the existing text of the book? Word processing equipment, of one kind or another, is now commonplace. Probably few revisers have to rely on making alterations to a copy of the previous edition. Deleting outdated text, with a red ink pen, is not too difficult. Making minor amendments in the same way may be tolerable. Stapling slips of paper, containing longer additions or alterations, to pages of the book makes life difficult for everybody concerned with making or editing the changes or typesetting the new edition.

Everybody benefits from the use of a word processor. There are two obvious ways of doing this:

1. The reviser transfers all the previous edition onto disk, amending the text as he does so.

2. A word processor operator transfers the unamended previous edition onto disk, and the updater amends the disk, using a compatible word processor.

Either of those methods would be preferable to the old ones. Doubtless more sophisticated systems will emerge during the next few years. Unless the amendments are made orally onto disk or tape, it seems likely that the person who makes them will use a method not too different from those outlined in this section.

Considering illustrations

When you check through the changes you have made in the text, think about illustrations. If the previous edition contained them, do they need updating? If there were none, would the addition of illustrations improve the book and increase its sales?

You will already have dealt with any that were within the text. They would include worked examples of arithmetical items, such as tax matters; also narrative examples, such as 'If A is bitten by B's dog . . .'.

Diagrams, charts and photographs may be as effective as they were when first included, but you should give them more than a cursory glance. A caption might benefit from an alteration, and the subject of the book or chapter might deserve a more recent photograph.

If the previous author included no illustrations, but you think they would enhance the value of the book, drop a line to the publisher. Explain what you have in mind and how you think the illustrations would improve the book.

TYING UP THE ENDS

When you are revising a book, the general principles that you have been considering while reading this book still apply, except to any extent that this chapter alters them.

When you have completed the revision, you send the typescript and any illustrations to the publisher, with a covering letter. The work of agreeing the text and proofs with the publisher's copy-editor will follow, as in Chapter 8.

Paying the piper

You may be revising a book that you wrote yourself. If so, the terms of the agreement that you signed before writing the original book will spell out your financial interest in the new edition. It probably consists of a royalty on the sales of the new edition at the same rates as on the old. Your reward for revising the book is that the book will probably continue to sell, instead of losing favour. If so, you will continue to receive royalty payments when they might have dried up.

If a publisher asked you to revise a book written by another author who was either unable or unwilling to do the job, the publisher would usually offer you a lump sum payment for making the revision.

CHECKLIST

● Have you listed all the points that your reading of the book identified as needing changing?

● Have you listed all the relevant changes that have occurred since the book was published?

● Have you amalgamated the contents of the two lists?

● Have you balanced the advantages and disadvantages of amending the book instead of rewriting it?

● Have you agreed with the publisher whether to amend or rewrite?

● If you are rewriting, have you replanned the layout?

● If you are amending, have you charted all the places where each relevant change needs to be taken into account?

● Have you polished the style and increased the clarity of the text while updating the data?

● Have you chosen the best 'equipment' for carrying out the alterations?

● Have you made the right decisions about illustrations?

CASE STUDIES

The case studies in the previous chapters all relate to authors who are writing new books. Because this chapter deals with updating existing books, the following case studies are about works by different authors from the usual four.

Sue updates a tax guide

Sue, a senior tax consultant, has recently taken over the work of a senior employee of a firm of Chartered Accountants who has retired. For many years he wrote and updated a tax guide bearing the firm's name. Sue was his deputy, and worked with him on the successive editions, as well as on his other duties. A new update is required, and Sue has been asked to write it. Because of her familiarity with the previous author's work, and the relatively minor extent of necessary changes, she decides to retain all of the previous edition that is still valid. She has no doubt that she can match her predecessor's style in the parts that need to be rewritten or created from scratch.

Tom suggests a new approach

Fifteen years ago before his death, Ernest Miller wrote his autobiography. His widow asks Tom to update the book, continuing the story to the date of Ernest's death. Tom points out that he could neither match Ernest's style nor creep into his mind and write convincingly in the first person singular. If he were provided with Ernest's diaries and introductions to the people he had known best in the years after the autobiography, he might write *Ernest's Later Years*. Whether the publisher of Ernest's work would be interested in this, Tom does not know. Ernest's widow visits the publisher, who shows an interest in the idea. He thinks it might create an opportunity for reprinting Ernest's work, with a foreword by Tom.

DISCUSSION POINTS

1. Is there any mileage in training oneself to copy other authors' style?

2. How likely is your book to run into a second edition?

8
Getting It Published

Banish any idea you may have that dotting your last 'i' and crossing your last 't' on the final page of the typescript is the end of your job. Your baby will need your parental help until it emerges in a bright glossy cover to take its place in the world. And anything you can go on doing, after that, to ensure that it isn't left on the shelf will increase its future prosperity.

SENDING OFF THE TYPESCRIPT

First things first! Before doing anything else, look at your contract again. Make sure you have done everything you need to do to satisfy its provisions. You have been busy with preparing the script. Have you overlooked anything else?

You may want to quote part of an Act of Parliament in an appendix. Have you obtained written authority to do so from Her Majesty's Stationery Office? What about permission to quote any other copyright material?

Presenting it correctly

If the publisher has sent you a copy of the house style, check that you have followed it, in your final revision of the script.

While publishers require scripts to be typed, and usually ask for double spacing on A4 paper, they do not normally stipulate pica or elite type size. They assume that it will be a generally acceptable size. Nor do they usually say how pages are to be numbered.

But numbering is clearly desirable. Imagine the effect of dropping an unnumbered script on the floor. Trying to put the pages back in order could be a mammoth task for you and almost impossible for a stranger.

You may be using a word processor with a facility for numbering pages. If not, number them legibly with a pencil, at the top right-hand corner. Number the copy you are going to keep in identical fashion.

That will make life easier if somebody wants to ask you a question about something in the script.

Prepare the number of copies of the script required, of the quality asked for, to be sent to the publisher.

Counting words

Your word processor may count the number of words in each chapter for you. If it has no such facility you need to make a good approximation. Counting the number of words in, say, 100 consecutive lines of typing may give you a fair figure for the average number of words in a line. By counting the numbers of lines in several pages, chosen at random, you can calculate the average numbers of lines and words on a page. Multiplying the latter by the number of pages in your script provides an approximate word count for the script.

Dispatching the typescript

Before starting to package the copies of the typescript, write to the publisher setting out any points you think you should mention. Include everything that you believe may help the staff in handling the book, such as a prior promise by you to prepare the index, in due course.

Collect all the illustrations, charts, diagrams and other items for insertion in spaces in the text. Make sure that they are clearly captioned. Bear in mind that the caption for any photographic print should preferably be written or typed on a label and stuck on the back of the print.

Transparencies require different treatment. Slot them into a display sheet, bought from a photographic shop, after numbering them on their mounts. Identify them by captions with the same numbers, typed on an accompanying sheet of paper. The display sheet has spaces for the insertion of several transparencies in plastic pockets. It enables the person responsible for designing the pages of the book to view them all at the same time, to decide which to use. For this purpose, the sheet is laid on an illuminated glass screen.

Packaging the work

It may be best to send the illustrations *etc* in a separate stiff envelope. A letter with them should then explain that they relate to the typescript, which is coming under separate cover. However, if the shape and size of the package containing the script is suitable, the stiff envelope may be included in the package containing the rest of the work.

After working on the book for so long, you want it to arrive at the publisher's premises in perfect condition. One of the boxes in which you buy your A4 paper is an excellent inner container for the typescript – possibly for both copies, clearly separated, if the publisher wants two. If it is too deep to hold the pages firmly, you can reduce the depth of both box and lid with the help of a steel ruler and a Stanley knife.

Remember to put your list of illustrations, contents page and preface on top of your pile of the chapters in the box. And stick a label, with the title and approximate length of the book and your name on it, on the top of the box.

Lay your letter on top of the box. Wrap the box firmly with strong brown paper and stick parcel tape over each overlap in the wrapping. Pay the correct fee to the Royal Mail or other parcel service you choose to deliver the package to the publisher.

LIAISING WITH THE PUBLISHER'S COPY-EDITOR

Before the work of converting your typescript into printed pages can begin, the publisher's copy-editor will go through it, noting anything that raises a query in his or her mind:

● 'Does the author really mean that?'

● 'Is this a jargon word I haven't met before?'

● 'Has something been missed out here?'

● 'Would it be better to say . . .?'

● 'I find this paragraph difficult to understand.'

There are many possible notes, depending on your experience of your role and the editor's familiarity with the subject of your book.

The copy-editor will probably write to you, listing the queries and the page number and location on the page of each item. Sometimes the editor's ignorance of the subject of the book accounts for all the queries.

If you have a fax number, the editor may use it. If the queries are few and minor, the editor may try to deal with them by phone. Usually it is better to have a record of both the query and the answer on paper.

In an extreme situation, an editor might wish to discuss a problem face to face. This would be unlikely, unless you lived or worked near the publisher's office.

The sooner the editor has a satisfactory reply to the queries, the sooner the work can go forward. But an over-hasty reply may slow up the process or lead to an error appearing in the book. This could be the result of your giving an unclear response to one of the queries.

WRITING A BLURB

At this stage, if not before, the publisher will ask you for a blurb, and will tell you the required length. A blurb is a short eulogy of you and your book. It summarises what the book will do for the reader and how well it will do it. It leaves no doubt that you are the ideal person to have written the book. It tells of your achievements, in glowing terms. It gives no indication that you have written the blurb as well as the book.

The publisher usually puts the blurb on the back cover of the book, or on a turned in part of the dust cover of a hardback book. It may also be used in the publisher's list of new books.

Throw your modesty out of the window before you start to write your blurb. You can retrieve it later.

CHECKING PROOFS

After finishing checking your typescript and adding any typesetting directions, the publisher's copyeditor passes it to the typesetter. If there are to be illustrations within the text, the designer takes over and plans the layout of the pages.

When the text has been set in page form, copies of the pages – referred to as page proofs – are read by the publisher's proofreader. He or she looks for typesetting and page-setting errors, and adds correction marks. These are in a standard form and used in accordance with a standard procedure registered with the British Standards Institution. You can see a copy in the *Writers' & Artists' Yearbook*.

Your proofreading role

Photocopies of the marked pages will be sent to you for further correction. The proofreader may not have been asked to compare the proofs with your text. Finding any departure from what you wrote usually depends on you. Being the author, you should be able to find any transcription errors quickly.

Speed is essential. Your contract probably imposes a time limit within which you must complete your checking of the proofs and return them to the publisher.

The time limit gives no scope for revising what you wrote. You should complete your revision before sending the script to the publisher. The contract includes a penalty clause to discourage any tampering with what you and the publisher's copyeditor have agreed.

Although your primary function in checking the proofs is to pick up any deviation by them from your typescript, you should not ignore any other error that may have been overlooked, such as a misspelling. Putting a marketable book in the shops is a team effort, and you are part of the team. Draw attention to any such other error.

INDEXING

Anybody who buys your book deserves to find a good index at the end of it. Is it likely that someone other than you would prepare the best index? No, surely not!

Nobody can complete the preparation of this feature until the type has been set and the pages have been numbered. But you can start working on the index sooner than anybody else.

Doing it yourself

You have kept a copy of the script. As soon as you have packaged the publisher's copy and other items, and dispatched them, you can direct your energies to preparing the index.

With a highlighting pen in your hand, read through the script and mark every word or phrase that you think should feature in the index.

Prepare a skeleton index. This could be an address book, with thumb tabs down the right-hand edges of the pages. Or you could use some sheets of ruled paper, writing A, B, C, *etc* at suitable intervals on the left-hand edges of the sheets.

Return to the script and enter the key word or phrase for each highlight mark in your skeleton index, and add the page number. For successive marks relating to the same key word or phrase, add the page number after the previous entry.

When you reach the end of the script, sort the information for each initial letter into alphabetical order.

Where there are alternative key words or phrases for a subject, the simplest system is to use a cross-reference. For example, in a book about religions, your list might include, 'Anglican, see Church of England', or a book about photography might include, 'colour slides, see transparencies'.

When you receive the copies of the page proofs from the publisher, checking them comes first. As soon as you have done that, you can lay the script and proofs side by side, and quickly find in the proofs each word and phrase you highlighted in the script. Delete the page number in the script from the index, and substitute the page number in the proofs.

Simplifying the task

If you use a word processor for your writing, creating the index can be easier. You need no thumb-notched book or loose ruled sheets. You can enter you key words and phrases in fully alphabetical order, from commencement.

As soon as you have substituted the page numbers in the proofs for those in the script, you have an index that you can print, and send to the publisher when returning the copy of the proofs, with any comments.

PUBLICISING YOUR BOOK

Which card can you play now to boost the sales of your book? If you have no ideas, start thinking. Your publisher will set the sales staff working in the interests of your book, but you might help them if you mentioned some facet of your life that they are unaware of.

Getting a plug

Do you know a leading light in something connected with your subject? If your book is about steam trains, do you know somebody who helps on the Bluebell Line? If it is about cricket, do you know a member of your local county cricket club? If you have written about a notorious crime of the past, do you know a former senior CID officer?

Whatever your subject may be, knowing somebody who has or had a connection with that subject may be an asset. You are looking for someone who could usefully write a foreword for your book. If the person you have in mind does not fill the bill, maybe he or she 'knows a man who can'.

Play this idea diplomatically. The last thing you want is a

reputation for making a convenience of your friends. You need somebody who would enjoy writing a foreword – not someone who would think of you as a scrounger.

If you find somebody suitable and willing, tell the publisher and show the volunteer your copy of the script so that he or she may write the foreword. When it has been written satisfactorily, send it to the publisher.

Other useful leads

Do you belong to a writers' group? If so, would one of the members write a news item for the local free newspaper about your book?

Do your employers have a house journal? The editor would probably like to know about the book. And some of your colleagues might buy a copy and ask you to autograph it.

The more you think along these lines, the more possibilities for promoting the book may occur to you.

AND FINALLY

If anything unforeseen that affects the accuracy of your book happens after you dispatch the script, advise the publisher immediately. If it is too late to add a note to the text, it may be possible to stick an amending slip in the copies of the book before issuing them.

CHECKLIST

● Have you checked that you have done all that the contract requires you to do?

● Does your covering letter include all the points you ought to mention to the publisher?

● Have you packaged the typescript, illustrations, letter and any other necessary enclosures securely, in a strong wrapper?

● Have you marked, on your copy of the script, all the items to be indexed?

● Have you prepared the index, as far as possible?

● Have you understood all the questions the publisher's copy-editor has asked?

● Have you answered them fully and clearly?

● Have you checked that the page proofs copy the script faithfully?

● Have you completed the index and sent it to the publisher?

● Have you identified and explored all the avenues you have for promoting sales of your book?

CASE STUDIES

Betty is too modest

Betty is satisfied that she has complied with the house style of the publisher. As a newcomer to the world of writing, she had paid close attention to it. Her job has taught her the art of packaging, and she has access to first class materials.

Writing a blurb is more of a problem. Although able to hold her own in the world of trade, she has difficulty in blowing her own trumpet. The publisher returns her first draft for rewriting, with the comment, 'Unless you tell people what a good writer you are *now*, they may never find out'. Her second effort gains the one-word comment, 'Excellent!'

The publisher's copyeditor has few queries about the text of the book, and Betty finds only one place where the page proofs differ from her script. The editor arranges for a professional indexer to relieve Betty of the task of preparing the index. But the shop she manages already exhibits advance publicity for the book, prominently.

Charles checks his own proofs

Having handed over the typescript and captioned illustrations to the publisher, in person, before reporting to his university, Charles arranges to check the proofs himself. He delegates indexing to Dick, and publicity to the charity for which Dick and he had made the sponsored walk.

Margaret does it by the book

Margaret kept the publisher's guidelines beside her while she worked on the typescript. She is confident that she has followed them. Her letter lists illustrations that she suggests the publisher might obtain from an agency and encloses sketches and charts she has drawn herself. She also offers to prepare the index. She arranges for a colleague to deliver the package containing the script, letter and other items to the publisher's office. While waiting for the proofs to arrive, Margaret marks up her copy of the script and sets up the skeleton index on her word processor.

In due course, she receives a letter from the publisher's copy-editor, rewrites two sentences to clarify their meaning, and answers the other queries. She checks the page proofs, points out half a dozen missettings of the text, and finishes the index. Finally, she writes to some of her college friends and other people she knows who are concerned with teaching the humanities, forewarning them of the publication of her book.

Tony concentrates on publicity

Production of the book is already well in hand. The designer has completed his last task, a dignified but colourful dust jacket that lacks only a blurb and a photograph of the author. Tony provides these and concentrates on his publicity role of setting up a programme for distributing the copies of the book.

DISCUSSION POINTS

1. Are there any writers' groups in your part of the UK who might ask you to give a talk on your experience of writing your book?

2. What plans have you for your next book?

Glossary

Administrator. Person who has been given legal power and responsibility for dealing with the estate of someone who has died without leaving a will, or without appointing an executor.

Advance. Payment sometimes made by a publisher, on signature of form of agreement and/or delivery of typescript, and deducted from royalties as they accrue.

Autobiography. Account of a person's life, or a selected part of it, written by that person.

Assign. Transfer one's rights in specified property to another person.

Assigns. People to whom property rights have been assigned.

Biography. Account of all or a selected part of a person's life, based on research and usually authorised by that person, or by his or her family or personal representatives. Where the person is long since deceased, no question of authority arises.

Blurb. An enthusiastic potted account of an author's relevant experience, used to promote the sale of the book and often written by the author.

Bullet point. A printed statement or question emphasised by being preceded by a large dot.

Contract. An agreement between parties, on mutually agreed and binding terms, for achieving a certain objective. (The word 'contract' is also used to mean the document containing details of the agreement.)

Copy-editor. Person who checks the author's typescript for sense and consistency and identifies headings, placement of illustrations *etc* in preparation for typesetting.

Copyright. The exclusive right to publish a particular work, such as a book, until 70 years after the death of the author.

Copywriter. Someone who writes the text of advertising material.

CV. Abbreviation of *curriculum vitae*, a Latin term for a summary of a person's educational and occupational qualifications.

Estate. A person's property.

Executor. Somebody appointed by a person making a will to deal with that person's estate after his or her death.

Form of agreement. Another name for a contract.

Ghosting. The writing of an ostensible autobiography by a person other than the subject of the book, who may give credit to the writer for having co-operated in the writing.

House style. The way in which a publisher wishes authors to set out their work.

ISBN. International Standard Book Number.

Libel. Publishing defamatory matter in a permanent form (which now includes radio and television).

Licence. Permission.

Liquidation. Winding up of a company.

Literary agent. Someone who acts on behalf of an author in dealings with publishers, in return for receiving a percentage of the author's royalties.

Out of print. Removed from the publisher's list.

Personal representatives. Executors and administrators.

Picture agency or library. Source of transparencies and other illustrations that may be borrowed for reproduction in a book, in return for payment of a fee.

Plagiarism. Appropriating other people's work.

Proofs. A printing of the typesetting of a book to facilitate finding errors in the typesetting.

Provisions. Statements that set out the terms of a document.

Publisher. The individual, partnership or company that owns a publishing house.

Reconstruction. The rebuilding of a commercial company – usually in a different setup from what preceded the change.

Royalty. A percentage of the takings from the sale of copies of a book or the leasing of rights in it.

Style sheet. A page containing details of a publisher's house style.

Synopsis. Summary of an author's ideas for a prospective book.

Text. The main body of the wording of a book either in draft or typeset form.

Title. (1) The name by which a book is known. (2) The right of the holder of property to deal with the property.

Typesetting. Preparing the master 'copy' of the author's text from which the pages of the book will be printed. (The word came from the old system in which letters and other characters, cast on tiny individual lead blocks, were set in a frame, by hand, to form the master copy.)

Unsolicited manuscript. Script sent to publisher without prior reference or invitation to submit.

Vanity publishing. Publication of a book at the author's expense.

Word processor. Equipment for the setting, storing and printing of words and other material by electronic means.

Useful Addresses

The Society of Authors, 84 Drayton Gardens, London SW10 9SB. Tel: (0171) 373 6642. The Society is a limited company, certified as an independent trade union (not affiliated to the TUC). Among other facilities, it helps writers in the following ways:

- Advising on negotiations (including clause by clause vetting of contracts).
- Taking up complaints on any issue concerned with the business of authorship.
- Pursuing legal actions for breach of contract, copyright infringement, *etc* (but not libel), when the risk and cost preclude individual action and an issue of general concern to authors is at stake.
- Supplying free of charge a quarterly journal, *The Author*, a unique source of information for authors – and a twice-yearly supplement, *The Electronic Author*.
- Publishing and supplying to members free of charge Quick Guides on Authors' Agents, Copyright and Moral Rights, The Protection of Titles, Copyright after your Death, Libel, Income Tax, VAT, Buying a Word-Processor, Permissions, Artistic Works and Photographs, The Small Claims Court, and Publishing Contracts. Also Guidelines for Authors of Educational Books, Guidelines for Authors of Medical Books, and Sell Your Writing.

Membership subscription – £65 per annum (reducible for payment by direct debit and for authors under 35 not yet earning significant income from writing.)

Contact: the Membership Secretary.

British Library Newspaper Library, Colindale Avenue, London NW9 5HE. Tel: (0171) 412 7353. The Library is a short walk from Colindale Station, London Transport Northern Line, Edgware train. A newspaper library day pass is available from the above address.

The library houses a large number of newspapers and weekly periodicals from all parts of the British Isles. Checking beforehand that what you wish to see would be available is a wise precaution.

Further Reading

The Writer's Handbook, annual, (Macmillan). In addition to listing UK, Irish, European and US publishers, with details of other interests, the book covers newspapers and magazines, radio and television, and literary agents. And it lists libraries and picture libraries.

There are articles about copyright and libel, debt collecting and paying taxes. There are also writers' courses, writers' circles and workshops. And there are details of many and varied professional associations.

The Writers' & Artists' Yearbook, annual, (A & C Black). Nearly 80 years older than *The Writer's Handbook*, this book covers much of the same ground but includes many articles that usefully supplement those in the younger book. These include valuable information about proofreading.

This book also provides details of publishers and societies of interest to people in other branches of the arts – such as theatre, photography and music. And it lists book publishers in British Commonwealth countries.

The Oxford English Grammar (Oxford University Press, 1996). For any writer whose schooling included traditional teaching about English grammar, this book provides a comprehensive analysis of a living language. It is more concerned with seeing how people speak and write than saying how they ought to speak and write.

The Oxford Writers' Dictionary (Oxford University Press, 1990).

Brewer's Dictionary of Phrase and Fable (Cassell).

Modern English Usage, Fowler (Oxford University Press).

The Oxford Dictionary of Quotations (Oxford University Press).

The Oxford Dictionary of English Proverbs (Oxford University Press).

Index